VIDEO EDITING WITH CAPCUT

Transforming Moments into Masterpieces, Elevate Your Story with CapCut's Enchanting Editing Tools. For beginners and professionals.

LIAM JOSEPH

TABLE OF CONTENTS

CHAPTER ONE

INTRODUCTION TO CAPCUT

CapCut stands out as an impressive and user-friendly video editing tool that is rapidly gaining popularity among content creators and influencers in the realm of social media. Developed by ByteDance, the Chinese technology company renowned for TikTok, CapCut provides a seamless editing experience through its intuitive interface and robust feature set. Regardless of whether you are a beginner venturing into video editing or an experienced professional seeking a streamlined process, CapCut offers everything you need to bring your creative ideas to life.

CapCut simplifies the video editing process by incorporating filters, transition effects, music, and other elements that enhance the appeal and creativity of the footage. Its editing toolbox encompasses fundamental features such as clip trimming, splitting, speed, and length adjustment, as well as transitions between clips. The software also offers a wide array of effects, including text, titles, stickers, emojis, glitch effects, and light leaks. For users desiring more advanced editing techniques, CapCut provides options like keyframe animation, color correction, masking, and blending modes. Additionally, users can import and edit audio files, adjust audio levels, and incorporate sound effects into their videos.

A notable feature of CapCut is its cost-free nature, devoid of watermarks or time limitations on videos. This makes it an ideal choice for individuals aiming to produce high-quality content on a budget.

CapCut caters to both novices and seasoned editors, thanks to its userfriendly interface and extensive library of training and support materials.

Further setting itself apart, CapCut incorporates AI-powered editing tools that automatically adjust video settings, such as brightness, contrast, and saturation, based on the video's content. This AI functionality proves invaluable for users looking to quickly enhance their videos without the need for manual parameter adjustments.

Whether creating content for social media, YouTube, or other platforms, CapCut emerges as a versatile and potent video editing solution. With its impressive capabilities, user-friendly design, and extensive support, CapCut empowers users to craft stunning videos that captivate audiences and establish a distinctive presence. Waste no time – download CapCut now and embark on the journey of creating visually appealing videos that set you apart from the rest.

BASIC FEATURES OF CAPCUT

CapCut stands out as a versatile and feature-packed video editing software, offering an extensive array of tools and effects to facilitate the creation of stunning and high-quality movies. Below are some of the key features that make CapCut a standout choice:

❖ **Basic editing tools**: CapCut incorporates fundamental editing functionalities, allowing users to effortlessly trim and split clips, adjust clip speed and duration, reverse video playback, and seamlessly incorporate transitions between clips. These user-friendly tools are designed to assist you in achieving a polished and fluid flow in your films with ease.

- ❖ **Effects and filters:** CapCut offers a diverse range of effects and filters, empowering users to infuse creative elements into their videos effortlessly. From text and titles to stickers, emojis, and unique effects such as glitch effects and light leaks, CapCut provides a user-friendly interface to enhance your videos with personality and flair. These intuitive filters and effects contribute to the overall creativity of your movies, making the process of adding visual appeal both straightforward and enjoyable.
- ❖ **Advanced editing techniques:** CapCut goes beyond basic editing with its advanced features, including keyframe animation, color correction, masking, and blending modes. These sophisticated tools provide users with enhanced control over their videos, enabling the creation of more intricate effects and seamless transitions. Whether you seek precise adjustments in animation, color grading, or intricate blending, CapCut's advanced editing capabilities cater to the needs of users looking to elevate the sophistication and creativity of their video projects.
- ❖ **Audio editing:** CapCut facilitates the import and editing of audio files, providing users with the capability to modify audio levels and incorporate sound effects seamlessly into their videos. This feature enhances the overall viewing experience, offering audiences a more immersive and engaging audio-visual presentation. By allowing for intricate audio customization, CapCut adds another layer of creativity, enabling users to craft videos that not only captivate visually but also deliver a rich and dynamic auditory experience.
- ❖ **Multi-layer editing:** CapCut boasts support for multiple layers in your videos, simplifying the process of adding and editing various features. This functionality allows you to effortlessly

incorporate text, stickers, and other elements into your video recordings. Additionally, the use of blending modes provides the opportunity to create intriguing effects, further enhancing the visual appeal of your videos. CapCut's multi-layer support offers users a versatile and dynamic editing environment, enabling the seamless integration of diverse elements to produce captivating and visually engaging content.

❖ **Video templates:** CapCut streamlines the video creation process by providing a variety of editable templates, enabling users to effortlessly produce professional-looking videos. These templates can be personalized with your text, photos, and videos, offering flexibility in content customization. Social media integration is a key feature of CapCut, ensuring seamless compatibility with platforms such as Instagram, TikTok, and YouTube. The app allows users to export videos in the correct format and size for these platforms, facilitating easy sharing directly from the application.

CapCut's extensive library of music and sound effects enhances the audio experience in videos. Users have the option to choose from the app's collection or import their music from their device's library.

Text overlays and stickers are easily incorporated into videos using CapCut, providing users with a variety of fonts and styles to choose from. This feature allows for creative expression and customization. The user-friendly interface of CapCut caters to both beginners and experienced video editors. With clear menus and controls, the app makes it easy to navigate and utilize the desired features. CapCut is offered as a free-to-use platform, devoid of watermarks or time limitations on videos. This affordability makes it an attractive option for individuals seeking to produce high-quality videos without incurring additional costs.

In summary, CapCut emerges as a powerful and versatile video editing app, equipped with an array of features and tools to facilitate the creation of stunning and professional-looking videos. Whether you're a novice or an experienced editor, CapCut provides all the necessary elements to bring your creative vision to life.

BENEFIT OF USING CAPCUT

CapCut stands out as a favored video editing app, providing a host of advantages for users, whether they are beginners or seasoned editors. Here are some of the key benefits of using CapCut:

- ❖ **Easy to use:** One of the biggest benefits of CapCut is its user-friendly interface. The app is designed to be easy to use, with clear menus and controls that make it easy to find and use the features you need. This makes it a great choice for novice video editors who are just starting.
- ❖ **Comprehensive editing tools:** CapCut provides a diverse set of editing tools that enable users to trim and split clips, adjust clip speed and duration, incorporate transitions and effects, and more. With comprehensive and versatile features, CapCut empowers users to create a wide array of video styles and effects, catering to a broad spectrum of creative needs.
- ❖ **Advanced editing features:** Beyond its basic editing tools, CapCut elevates the editing experience with advanced features such as keyframe animation, color correction, masking, and blending modes. These advanced capabilities provide users with heightened control over their videos, enabling the creation

of intricate effects and seamless transitions. With these features, CapCut caters to users seeking a more nuanced and sophisticated approach to video editing.

❖ **High-quality effects and filters:** CapCut provides a selection of high-quality effects and filters that can impart a professional touch to your videos. With options to add text, titles, stickers, emojis, and special effects like glitch effects and light leaks, CapCut makes it easy to enhance your videos with a touch of personality and style. These effects are user-friendly, offering a seamless way to elevate the visual appeal of your content.

❖ **Customizable templates:** CapCut further enhances user convenience by offering customizable templates that facilitate the swift and effortless creation of professional-looking videos. These templates are designed to be adaptable, allowing users to personalize them by adding their text, photos, and videos, ensuring a unique and tailored result. This feature streamlines the video creation process, making it accessible for users seeking a quick and easy way to produce polished and personalized content.

❖ **Social media integration:** CapCut is meticulously crafted to seamlessly integrate with popular social media platforms such as Instagram, TikTok, and YouTube. The app simplifies the sharing process by allowing users to export their videos in the appropriate format and size for these platforms. Moreover, CapCut goes a step further, enabling users to share their videos directly from the app, streamlining the workflow, and enhancing the efficiency of content distribution on various social media channels.

❖ **Free to use:** CapCut stands out as a cost-effective solution, being entirely free to use without imposing watermarks or time limitations on your videos. This makes it an ideal choice for individuals seeking to produce high-quality content without incurring additional expenses. CapCut's affordability enhances its appeal, offering a budget-friendly option for those looking to create professional and engaging videos without financial constraints.

❖ **Professional-quality results:** CapCut's extensive array of editing tools, coupled with high-quality effects and filters, as well as customizable templates, simplifies the process of crafting professional-quality videos. Whether you're creating a personal video or developing a promotional piece for your business, CapCut provides the features necessary to achieve the polished and professional look you desire. With its user-friendly interface and versatile toolkit, CapCut caters to a broad range of video creation needs, ensuring a seamless and professional outcome regardless of the context or purpose.

In conclusion, CapCut stands out as a versatile and user-friendly video editing application, providing an extensive range of features and tools to facilitate the creation of impressive and professional-quality videos. Whether you are a novice exploring video editing for the first time or an experienced editor seeking advanced capabilities, CapCut caters to all levels of expertise, offering a comprehensive suite of features to bring your creative vision to life with ease.

CHAPTER TWO

GET STARTED WITH CAPCUT

CapCut, a free and user-friendly video editing app, has recently gained prominence in both the Apple App Store and Google Play Store. Developed by the creators of TikTok, this app allows users to create captivating videos with just a few simple touches. In this post, we'll delve into its key features and impressive effects.

If you're an avid content creator on platforms like TikTok and seek a video editor that is both feature-rich and easy to use on Android or iPhone, CapCut is likely to become your favorite tool.

In a world where videos are ubiquitous, the ability to quickly and skillfully edit videos has become a valuable skill. CapCut, created by the team behind TikTok, enables users to seamlessly edit videos with impressive results. This app stands out for its capability to turn snippets into complete movies in an instant, incorporating visual effects that might typically be associated with professional video editing software. The creative possibilities it opens up may leave you amazed at how effortlessly users can craft imaginative and polished films.

WHAT CAN I USE CAPCUT FOR?

CapCut is perfect for a wide range of video creation. Let's explore how CapCut can be beneficial for each of these categories:

❖ **How to Videos:**

- CapCut's user-friendly interface and comprehensive editing tools make it an excellent choice for creating step-by-step how-to videos.
- The app's ability to add text, stickers, and effects can enhance instructional content, making it more engaging and informative.
- With features like speed adjustment and transitions, you can ensure your how-to videos are paced well and visually appealing.

❖ **Advertising, Marketing, and Promotions:**
- CapCut's customizable templates allow for the quick creation of professional-looking promotional videos.
- Advanced editing features, such as keyframe animation and blending modes, provide flexibility for creating unique and attention-grabbing marketing content.
- The app's compatibility with social media platforms makes it easy to tailor and share promotional videos across different channels.

❖ **Intro Videos:**
- CapCut's high-quality effects and filters can be utilized to craft eye-catching intro videos.
- The app's support for various layers enables users to add text, stickers, and other elements to create personalized and memorable intros.
- CapCut's seamless integration with social media platforms facilitates sharing captivating intros with your audience.

❖ **E-commerce:**
- CapCut's video editing capabilities are beneficial for creating product demonstration videos or showcasing your e-commerce offerings.

- The app's audio editing tools and extensive music library allow for the addition of background music or voiceovers to enhance e-commerce videos.
- Its compatibility with various video formats ensures that your e-commerce videos are suitable for different platforms.

CapCut's versatility, ease of use, and robust feature set make it a valuable tool for creating a wide range of videos across different categories, including how-to guides, advertising, intros, and e-commerce content.

WHO IS CAPCUT PERFECT FOR?

CapCut is perfect for anyone who wants to create videos, regardless of the type of video they are creating. CapCut is ideal for:

- ❖ Marketing professionals
- ❖ Casual creators
- ❖ Experienced creators
- ❖ TikTok creators

WHY USE CAPCUT?

As previously stated, there is a plethora of video editing and creation tools accessible. So, what sets CapCut apart? The mobile and desktop applications are exceptionally user-friendly, ensuring that video creation is not only enjoyable but also more straightforward than ever. The applications boast a myriad of features, catering to individuals creating general videos intended for social media use. Notably, the stickers, effects, and music libraries within CapCut are highly commendable, offering extensive options for personalizing your videos.

HOW TO DOWNLOAD AND INSTALL CAPCUT

Downloading and installing CapCut is a straightforward process. Developed as a mobile application for both iOS and Android smartphones, CapCut is exclusively designed to enhance the core video editing functionalities of the widely-used social media platform, TikTok. Marketed as a free TikTok editing app, CapCut can be downloaded at no cost. Its comparable features on both iOS and Android platforms empower users to edit their TikTok videos with a range of enhancements, including filters, stickers, speed adjustments, background music, effects, and more. Additionally, CapCut provides advanced editing options such as split and reverse to elevate the overall appearance of your TikTok videos, giving them a polished and professional touch. To guide you through the process, here's how to get started:

Downloading And Installation For Andriod

Steps:

- ❖ Begin by launching the Google Play Store on your Android device.
- ❖ In the search bar, type "CapCut" to locate the application.
- ❖ Click on the "Install" button to initiate the downloading and installation process.
- ❖ Patiently wait for the app to be downloaded and installed on your device.

❖ Upon completion of the installation, open the CapCut app and proceed to sign up for a new account.

Downloading And Installation For Ios Devices:

❖ Initiate the process by accessing the App Store on your iOS device.
❖ Utilize the search bar to look for "CapCut."
❖ Select the "Get" button to commence the downloading and installation of the app.
❖ Allow the app to download and install on your iOS device, exercising patience during this process.
❖ Following the completion of the installation, launch the CapCut app and proceed to sign up for a new account.

Upon successfully downloading and installing the app, the next step involves signing up for a new account to begin utilizing its features. Registration can be accomplished using either your phone number or email address. Once the sign-up process is completed, you gain access to CapCut's extensive editing tools, along with its impressive array of high-quality effects and filters, enabling you to commence the creation and editing of videos with ease.

HOW TO CREATE A NEW PROJECT ON CAPCUT

Initiating a new project in CapCut is a straightforward process. Follow these steps:

❖ Open the CapCut app on your mobile device.
❖ On the home screen, tap on the "new project" or "+" icon located at the bottom.

- ❖ Choose the aspect ratio for your project, with options like 16:9, 9:16, 1:1, and more.
- ❖ Select a video or image to incorporate into your project, and you can opt for multiple media files.
- ❖ After adding your media, utilize CapCut's editing tools to customize your project. This includes tasks such as trimming and splitting clips, incorporating music and sound effects, adjusting color and lighting, and more.
- ❖ Once your editing is complete, export the project to save it on your device or share it on social media.

In essence, creating a new project in CapCut is both rapid and uncomplicated. Leveraging the app's potent editing tools ensures the swift production of high-quality videos.

HOW TO OPEN AN EXISTING PROJECT IN CAPCUT

To access an existing project in CapCut, adhere to these uncomplicated steps:

- ❖ Open the CapCut app on your mobile device.
- ❖ On the home screen, select the "Projects" tab situated at the bottom.
- ❖ A list of all your created projects in CapCut will be visible. Locate the specific project you wish to open and tap on it.
- ❖ The project will open, allowing you to resume editing or exporting according to your preferences.

Should you encounter difficulty locating your project, utilize the search bar at the top of the Projects screen to search by name. Additionally, you can organize your projects by date or name for easier identification.

opening an existing project in CapCut is a simple process, and once you've located your project, you can seamlessly continue refining and editing it using the app's robust tools.

UNDERSTANDING CAPCUT INTERFACE

CapCut's interface is thoughtfully designed to cater to both beginners and advanced users, offering a user-friendly and intuitive experience for crafting high-quality videos. Here's an in-depth overview of the CapCut interface:

❖ **Home Screen:** The home screen serves as the app's main hub, providing access to all projects, templates, featured content, and the option to initiate a new project.

❖ **Project Screen:** Upon opening or creating a project, users are directed to the project screen. This interface facilitates the management of all media assets within the project, including videos, photos, and audio tracks. Various editing tools such as filters, effects, and transitions can be accessed from this screen.

❖ **Editing Interface:** The editing interface is where the majority of video editing takes place, consisting of key elements:

• Timeline: Arrange and edit video clips, audio tracks, and other elements on the timeline to create the final video.

• Toolbar: Located at the bottom, the toolbar houses all necessary editing tools for adding text, music, transitions, effects, and more.

• Preview Window: Displaying a real-time preview of the edited video, the preview window allows users to visualize changes instantly.

- Asset Library: All imported media files, such as video clips, photos, music, and sound effects, are stored in the asset library, accessible via the icon in the upper-left corner.
- ❖ **Editing Tools:** CapCut offers a diverse set of editing tools and features to enhance video content:
  - Filters: Apply a variety of filters to give the video a specific look or style.
  - Effects: Incorporate motion graphics, text, and other visual elements using CapCut's assortment of effects.
  - Transitions: Smoothly transition between different video clips with a selection of transitions.
  - Audio Editing: Add, edit, and mix audio tracks within the project. Sound effects can be included, and voiceovers can be recorded directly within the app.
- ❖ **Exporting:** After completing the editing process, users can export the video, save it to their device, or share it on social media. CapCut provides various export options, including different video formats and resolutions. Direct sharing to platforms like TikTok and Instagram is also supported.

In conclusion, CapCut's interface is not only user-friendly but also packed with tools and features that facilitate the creation of professional-looking videos on mobile devices. Whether you're a novice or an experienced user, CapCut provides a comprehensive suite of tools for crafting engaging videos.

CHAPTER THREE

CAPCUT WORKSPACE

The CapCut workspace is meticulously crafted to offer users a user-friendly and accessible environment for video editing, featuring a diverse set of tools and features that simplify the creation of professional-looking videos. This section will delve into the various components that constitute the CapCut workspace.

COMPONENTS OF CAPCUT WORKSPACE

CapCut workspace comprises several components that are essential for creating and editing videos. These components include the media library, timeline, preview window, and various editing tools.

The media library provides access to all the media files such as videos, images, and audio clips that can be used in the project. The timeline is where users can arrange and edit their media files, and add transitions, effects, and music. The preview window allows users to view their projects in real time as they edit.

In addition, CapCut also provides various editing tools, including text overlays, filters, stickers, and animations that can be added to the video to enhance its quality. Overall, the combination of these components makes CapCut a powerful video editing tool that is accessible to both novice and professional video editors.

Timeline

The timeline holds a crucial role within the CapCut workspace, serving as a central hub for users to add and edit video clips, audio, and effects. Functioning as a visual representation of the video project, it presents the various elements in chronological order.

❖ **Timeline Navigation**: CapCut's timeline navigation is designed with user-friendly and intuitive features, enabling users to navigate through their projects with ease and efficiency.

The timeline navigation in CapCut incorporates diverse features that enhance its user-friendliness. Users have the capability to zoom in and out of the timeline, providing a clearer view of their projects. This functionality proves particularly beneficial when

working on intricate videos containing multiple clips and effects.

Another valuable feature in CapCut's timeline navigation is the capability to move the playhead to a specific point in the timeline. This empowers users to effortlessly locate and edit specific clips or add transitions and effects with precision.

The playhead serves as a crucial element in CapCut's timeline navigation, represented by a vertical line indicating the current playback position. Users have the flexibility to drag the playhead to any point in the timeline, facilitating the precise addition of effects and transitions or the location of specific clips. Additionally, the playhead enables users to preview their video in real-time, ensuring a seamless flow in the final result.

CapCut further enhances user flexibility by providing the option to split clips, a valuable feature for users looking to divide a single clip into two sections or eliminate unwanted footage. Additionally, users can fine-tune the duration of a clip, assisting in aligning clip lengths with the music or narration. The timeline navigation in CapCut facilitates the adjustment of a clip's duration, a useful functionality for harmonizing clip lengths with music or narration. Users can achieve this adjustment by tapping on the clip and dragging its endpoint to the desired location.

CapCut's timeline navigation is meticulously crafted to be intuitive and user-friendly, empowering users to create high-quality videos effortlessly. With its array of features and capabilities, it proves to be an excellent tool catering to both novice and professional video editors alike.

❖ **Adding and Deleting Clips:** Adding video clips, audio, and images to the timeline in CapCut is a straightforward process accomplished by either dragging and dropping them from the media library or utilizing the "add media" button. Once added, users have the flexibility to trim, split, and rearrange clips as necessary. Deleting a clip is equally simple, requiring users to select the clip and press the delete key on their keyboard.

Within CapCut, the fundamental process of adding and deleting clips from the timeline is integral to video editing. This essential procedure enables users to select specific video segments, arranging them in the desired order to craft a comprehensive and cohesive video.

- **How to add a clip**

To incorporate a new clip into your timeline on CapCut, locate and click on the "+" button positioned in the bottom left corner of the screen. This action will prompt a menu, offering you the option to import clips from your camera roll or directly from your device's camera.

Upon selecting your preferred clip, it will be displayed on the timeline, allowing you to adjust its position to the desired location.

- **How to delete a clip**

Just click on the video you wish to erase and select the "Delete" option that displays to get rid of it.

Clicking on a clip and dragging it to the trash can icon on the left side of the screen is another method for deleting it. By moving your mouse over many clips at once and then erasing them all at once, you may also pick several clips at once.

It's important to note that deleting a clip from your timeline will not delete it from your camera roll or device storage. Therefore, A clip you've previously erased can always be reimported.

All in all, Capcut's clip addition and deletion features make it easy to personalize your movie timeline.

❖ **Adjusting Clip Length:** A clip's length may be changed by users by sliding its borders inside or outward. This comes in handy when cutting a clip to fit a certain length or editing the beginning or end of a clip. You may change the duration of individual video clips on your timeline by adjusting the clip length in Capcut, which is a crucial feature. By cutting or expanding the duration of a clip, you can adjust the tempo of your video and make it more appealing to your viewers.

A clip must first be selected by tapping on it in the timeline to change its duration. Next, you may adjust the clip's length by dragging its terminus farther or closer to the timeline's center. To fine-tune the duration even more, you may also utilize the slider at the bottom of the screen.

Using the "Split" tool provides another method of adjusting the clip length. With the help of this tool, you may split a video into two halves and edit either the beginning or the conclusion of the video separately. Choose the clip on the timeline, then press the scissors symbol above it to utilize the "Split" tool. After that, touch the scissors once again after dragging the slider to the desired split point for the clip.

By selecting multiple clips at once and dragging their ends to a different spot, you may also change the duration of each clip simultaneously. If you want to change the time of several clips at once, this is helpful.

With Capcut, modifying the clip length is a simple, quick, and effortless procedure. With the help of this feature, you may precisely edit your video to produce a more interesting and useful end product.

❖ **Layers:** Layering is another feature of CapCut's timeline that lets users arrange different audio and video clips on top of one another.

This makes more intricate editing possible, such as the ability to add text overlays and produce picture-in-picture effects. When editing videos, layers are a crucial tool since they let you combine various aspects to get a more dynamic and captivating result. Layers in Capcut allow you to embellish your film with text, stickers, pictures, and other effects. In Capcut, you must first choose the clip or picture to which you wish to apply a layer. Next, give the "Layers" symbol in the upper right corner of the screen a tap. From here, you have access to a wide range of layer choices, including Text, Effects, Stickers, and more. After choosing your preferred layer, you may modify its size, opacity, location, and other attributes.

Being able to modify a layer's location and timing on the timeline is one of Capcut's most helpful capabilities. This lets you overlay many layers and move them around over time to create intricate effects and animations. For instance, you may add a sticker that slides across the screen at specific points in your movie, or make a text layer that appears and vanishes over a specific clip.

Capcut not only lets you create and modify layers, but it also lets you group layers together for simpler layer management. Choose the layers you wish to join together and then press the "Group" icon. Tapping on the "Ungroup" icon will also allow you to ungroup layers.

All things considered, layers are a crucial component of Capcut's functionality as they let you incorporate a variety of effects and animations into your films. Capcut's user-friendly interface and strong layering features make it simple to produce captivating and dynamic movies that will hold the interest of your viewers.

❖ **Audio Editing:** The timeline allows users to edit the audio tracks in their videos by adjusting the volume and adding effects. Additionally, users may modify the timing of the music and add sound effects to complement the visual features of the movie.

With the use of CapCut's many audio editing capabilities, users may produce audio for their videos that are of a high caliber. CapCut offers the following capabilities for audio editing:

- Audio Import: Users of CapCut may import audio files from online storage services like Dropbox and Google Drive, as well as from the device's library. The audio file may be added to the timeline when it has been imported and is visible in the media library.

- Audio Editing Tools: A range of audio editing capabilities, such as audio split, fade in/out, and volume control, are available with CapCut. With the use of these technologies, consumers may provide their films with a smooth audio experience.

- Audio Effects: To improve the quality of audio recordings, CapCut also offers a range of audio effects, including distortion, reverb, and echo.

- Audio Recording: With the voice recording option offered by CapCut, users may record their voices or sound effects and import them straight into the program.

- Audio Syncing: Moreover, CapCut features a tool that lets users sync audio and video, which makes it simple to produce professional-caliber films with excellent audio.

❖ **Effects and Transitions:** The timeline in CapCut facilitates the incorporation of visual effects and seamless transitions between clips. Users may apply transitions between clips by picking the desired transition from the effects library and dragging it onto the timeline between two clips.

Users may add a range of effects and transitions to their films using CapCut to enhance their visual appeal and make them more captivating. The following are a some of the effects and transitions that CapCut offers:

- Filters: Videos may be edited with a variety of CapCut filters to alter their color and tone. Black & white, vintage, and cinematic are some of these filters.
- Text: To add titles, captions, and subtitles to videos, CapCut offers a variety of text possibilities. The text's font, size, color, and positioning are all customizable by the user.
- Stickers: A vast assortment of stickers from CapCut may be used to enhance and personalize films. Emojis, animated stickers, and 3D stickers are among these stickers.
- Transitions: A range of transition effects are available in CapCut that may be used to seamlessly transition between two video segments. These consist of slide, cross dissolve, and fade in/out.
- Animations: CapCut provides animation effects that can be used to add dynamic movements to text, stickers, and other elements in a video. These animations include scale, rotation, and fade in/out.
- Speed Control: Users may change the pace of their video clips with CapCut's speed control function. You may use this function to make time-lapse or slow-motion effects.

With CapCut's effects and transitions, users may enhance and enthrall audiences with their videos in a multitude of ways. Making professional-looking films doesn't need users to have a lot of video editing experience because the program has easy-to-use and configurable editing tools.

- ❖ **Keyframes:** Users can introduce keyframes to video clips and audio tracks within the timeline, allowing for the creation of distinct effects. These effects may include actions like zooming in or out of a video clip, adjusting the opacity of an image, or applying filters to a clip. To incorporate keyframes, users can choose the desired clip or audio track and click on the designated "keyframe" icon.

Within CapCut, users can employ keyframes to introduce animation effects and transitions to their videos. These keyframes serve the purpose of modifying values associated with different parameters—such as position, scale, opacity, and color—across the course of the video, offering a dynamic and engaging visual experience.

In CapCut, incorporating a keyframe is a straightforward process. Initially, choose the desired clip or layer for editing. Proceed to the keyframe icon situated in the top left corner of the editing screen. Within this interface, you can specify the parameter for which you wish to add a keyframe, such as position or scale. Upon selecting the parameter, a small diamond-shaped icon will materialize on the timeline, precisely marking the current time position.

After placing the initial keyframe, users can move the playhead to a different point in the timeline and modify the chosen parameter to a new value. CapCut will seamlessly integrate a new keyframe into the timeline, facilitating a smooth transition between the two values over time.

Furthermore, users possess the capability to fine-tune the interpolation type between keyframes, offering options like linear, bezier, and ease-in/ease-out. These choices provide enhanced control over the animation process, allowing for the creation of distinctive effects.

Beyond adjusting individual parameters, users can also utilize keyframes to apply effects and filters progressively to their videos. This feature empowers the creation of dynamic visual effects and transitions, enhancing the overall engagement and excitement of the video.

keyframes serve as a potent tool in CapCut, empowering users to craft intricate animations and transitions with precise control over both time and parameters.

In summary, the timeline within CapCut's workspace emerges as a robust and adaptable tool for video editing. It equips users with the capability to edit, trim, and rearrange clips, integrate audio and visual effects, and fine-tune the timing of both video and audio components. This comprehensive functionality ensures the creation of a refined and professional final product.

Media Library

The media library serves as a repository where users can retrieve their media files, including video clips, music, and sound effects. It enables users to import media either from their device's gallery or CapCut's integrated library.

Positioned conveniently at the bottom of the workspace, CapCut's media library is a potent tool, providing users with a seamless means to explore and incorporate media files from their devices directly into their projects. Its accessibility enhances the overall user experience.

The media library in CapCut is organized into several tabs, each categorizing media files based on their type. These tabs include "Videos," "Images," "Music," "Stickers," "Fonts," "Transitions," and "Effects." The "Videos" and "Images" tabs encompass all video and image files on the device, while the "Music" tab houses music files. The tabs for stickers, fonts, transitions, and effects contain various elements that can enhance video projects.

To incorporate a media file into your project, you can click on the file in the media library and drag it onto the timeline. Alternatively, selecting the file and choosing the "Insert" option adds the file to the timeline at the playhead's position.

CapCut's media library features a search function, facilitating quick retrieval of specific media files by name or tags. Additionally, the library allows users to import media directly from the internet by entering a URL for a video or audio file. CapCut will then automatically download and integrate the file into the project.

CapCut's media library is a vital aspect of the app, simplifying the process of browsing and importing media files into your project. With its user-friendly interface and robust capabilities, you can efficiently locate the needed media files and commence the creation of impressive videos.

Effects and Filters

CapCut provides users with a diverse range of effects and filters to elevate the visual appeal of their videos. These effects encompass transitions, color grading options, and special features such as slow motion and time-lapse. Users have the flexibility to apply these effects either to specific clips or to the entire video, allowing for creative and customized video enhancements.

How to apply effect or filter

To implement an effect or filter, you can effortlessly drag and drop it onto the desired clip in the timeline. For further customization, users can fine-tune the intensity of the effect or filter by utilizing the slider available in the editing panel. This intuitive process allows for easy and precise adjustments to achieve the desired visual impact. Some of the popular effects and filters available in CapCut include:

CapCut provides a diverse array of effects and filters, each serving a distinct purpose in enhancing your video content:

- ❖ **Color Correction:** Adjust the color balance, brightness, and contrast to correct any color issues in your video, resulting in a more natural appearance.
- ❖ **Blur:** Soften the edges of your footage with the blur effect, creating a dreamy ambiance and enabling focus on specific subjects in the video.
- ❖ **Glitch:** Add a distorted, fragmented look to your footage, providing a retro or futuristic aesthetic to your video.
- ❖ **Vintage:** Apply the vintage effect to give your video a classic, retro appearance, fostering a nostalgic or old-fashioned atmosphere.
- ❖ **Bokeh:** Create a cinematic feel by utilizing the bokeh effect, which produces a soft, out-of-focus background.

Alongside these effects, CapCut offers a variety of filters for further enhancing your video footage. These filters range from basic options like black and white and sepia to more advanced choices like HDR and film grain. In summary, CapCut's effects and filters provide a broad spectrum of options to elevate your video content, allowing for a unique and personalized look and feel.

Text and Titles

CapCut provides a comprehensive text and title editor, empowering users to incorporate text overlays and titles into their videos with customization options such as fonts, styles, and animations.

The text and title features in CapCut offer a diverse set of options for adding professional-looking text to your videos. These features encompass various fonts, sizes, colors, and text animation effects.

To integrate text into your video, navigate to the "Text" option in the bottom menu. Here, you can choose from pre-designed text templates or craft your customized text using the "Custom" option. Adjustments to font, size, color, and position on the screen can be made, and dynamic animation effects like fades, fly-ins, and zoom-ins can be applied for a more engaging presentation.

Beyond text, CapCut extends its capabilities with a range of title templates, enabling users to incorporate polished title sequences into their videos. These templates cover diverse video types, including travel, fashion, and vlogs, and are adaptable to meet specific requirements.

To add a title, select the "Title" option from the bottom menu. Choose from pre-designed title templates or create a custom title using the "Custom" option. After selecting your title, customize its font, size, color, and animation effects to seamlessly align with your video's theme and style.

In summary, CapCut's text and title features offer a broad spectrum of customization options, empowering users to craft professional-looking videos enriched with high-quality text and title sequences.

Audio Editing

CapCut offers an array of audio editing tools designed to empower users in adjusting audio volume, incorporating sound effects, and applying filters to enhance overall sound quality. Additionally, users can integrate their music or explore CapCut's built-in music library. Here are some key features of CapCut's audio editing capabilities:

❖ **Volume Adjustment:** Users can finely tune the volume of their audio clips. By selecting the audio clip on the timeline, tapping the speaker icon, and adjusting the slider, users can effortlessly increase or decrease the volume.

❖ **Fade In/Out:** For creating seamless transitions within audio clips, users can implement fade-in/out effects. By selecting the audio clip, tapping the speaker icon, and opting for "Fade In" or "Fade Out," users can achieve smooth transitions.

❖ **Audio Effects:** CapCut presents a variety of audio effects to enhance audio quality. By selecting the audio clip, tapping the speaker icon, and choosing "Audio Effect," users gain access to an array of effects like reverb, chorus, and distortion.

❖ **Audio Mixing:** In projects with multiple audio tracks, the audio mixing feature enables users to balance track levels and apply effects. Accessible by tapping the "Audio Mixing" icon at the bottom, users can adjust volumes and add effects to individual tracks.

❖ **Audio Sync:** CapCut provides an audio sync feature, particularly useful for projects where video and audio are recorded separately. To sync audio with video, users can select the video clip on the timeline, tap the speaker icon, and choose the "Sync Audio" option, adjusting the timing as needed.

These features represent only a fraction of the audio editing capabilities within CapCut. With these tools, users can elevate the audio quality of their projects, contributing to the creation of professional-quality videos.

Exporting and Sharing

After completing the video editing process, users can export their projects in multiple formats and resolutions, such as 1080p and 4K. Furthermore, CapCut facilitates seamless sharing by enabling users to directly post their videos on popular social media platforms like Instagram, TikTok, and YouTube.

In subsequent discussions, we will delve deeper into the intricacies of the exporting and sharing functionalities. All in all, CapCut's workspace offers users a potent and user-friendly space for video editing. With its extensive array of tools and features, users can produce top-notch videos without the necessity of costly equipment or professional training.

CHAPTER FOUR

MEDIA IN CAPCUT

CapCut stands out as a versatile video editing application, offering an extensive array of features and tools for users aiming to craft professional-looking videos. Among its pivotal components is the media library, a hub that grants users access to a diverse range of media files to incorporate into their projects.

In the context of CapCut, "media" encompasses various file types eligible for import, editing, and utilization in projects. These encompass video clips, images, audio files, and music tracks. CapCut's user-friendly interface facilitates the seamless addition and organization of media files within the designated Media section of the application.

Accessing the Media section involves tapping the "Media" button positioned at the screen's bottom, unveiling the media library. Here, users can navigate through their device's files to locate the desired media for their projects. Once identified, adding the media to the project involves selecting it and tapping the "Add" button, subsequently incorporating it into the project's media library for easy retrieval and utilization.

Beyond importing media from device files, CapCut enhances its offerings with built-in media, including music tracks, sound effects, and video effects. Users can access these resources by tapping the "Library" button within the Media section, revealing an assortment of pre-existing media that can seamlessly integrate into projects.

media plays a pivotal role in the realm of video editing, and CapCut elevates the experience by providing a wealth of options for adding, organizing, and effectively leveraging media in projects. Subsequent sections will delve into the distinct types of media available on CapCut and offer insights into maximizing their utility.

DIFFERENT TYPE OF MEDIA IN CAPCUT

CapCut accommodates various types of media, providing users with a versatile toolkit to enhance their video editing projects. The supported media types in CapCut include:

❖ **Video:** This is the primary and fundamental media type in CapCut. Users can import and edit video clips of diverse formats and resolutions, arranging them on the timeline to craft their projects.

❖ **Audio:** CapCut empowers users to import and edit audio files, enabling the creation of dynamic soundtracks for their videos. Users can seamlessly incorporate background music, sound effects, and voiceovers into their projects.

❖ **Images:** CapCut extends its capabilities to image editing, allowing users to import and modify images. This feature proves handy for crafting engaging photo slideshows or integrating graphics into video projects.

❖ **Text:** CapCut incorporates a suite of text tools, granting users the ability to add titles, captions, and various text elements to their videos. This enhances the communicative and storytelling aspects of the projects.

❖ **Effects:** CapCut offers an extensive array of visual effects, encompassing filters, transitions, and animations. Users can leverage these effects to elevate the visual appeal and storytelling dynamics of their videos.

❖ Stickers: CapCut includes a library of stickers and animated emojis, injecting a playful and creative dimension into videos. Users can utilize these stickers to add fun and unique elements to their video content.

By supporting this diverse range of media types, CapCut empowers users to unleash their creativity, resulting in engaging and professional-looking video projects. Subsequent sections will delve into the specifics of each media type and offer insights into their optimal utilization.

HOW TO IMPORT THE DIFFERENT TYPE OF MEDIA

We are going to talk about how to import video, audio, and images.

Understanding how to import video

To incorporate videos into your CapCut project, adhere to these steps:

❖ **Open CapCut:** Open the CapCut app and locate the plus icon positioned at the bottom center of the screen.

❖ **Select "Video":** Opt for the "Video" option from the presented choices.

❖ **Choose Import Source:** Specify the source from which you intend to import the video. Options include your phone's gallery, Google Drive, or Dropbox.

❖ **Preview and Selection:** After choosing the desired video(s), tap on it to preview the content.

❖ **import to CapCut:** If contentment prevails with the selected video(s), proceed to tap "Import" to integrate it into your CapCut project.

It's crucial to be aware that CapCut exclusively supports particular video formats such as MP4, AVI, MOV, and FLV. In instances where your video does not conform to these formats, conversion may be necessary before importing it into CapCut.

Understanding how to import how to import audio

To import videos and add audio on CapCut, follow these steps:

❖ **Open CapCut:** Launch the CapCut app on your device.
❖ **Create a New Project:** Tap on the "+" icon at the bottom of the screen to initiate a new project.
❖ **Select Video Clip:** Choose the video clip to which you want to add audio and tap on it.
❖ **Access Music Options:** Tap on the "Music" icon located at the bottom of the screen.
❖ **Choose Music Source:** You can opt for music from CapCut's library or tap on "My Music" to select music from your device's library.
❖ **Preview and Selection:** After choosing your desired audio track, tap on it to preview the selection.
❖ **Confirm and Add:** If content with your choice, tap on "Use" to integrate it into your video clip.

It's noteworthy that CapCut supports various audio formats such as MP3, M4A, AAC, and WAV.

Understanding how to import images in capcut

To import images into CapCut, follow these steps:

❖ **Open CapCut:** Open the CapCut app and either create a new project or open an existing one.

❖ **Access Media Library:** Click on the "Media" button located at the bottom of the screen.

❖ **Choose Image Source:** Choose the source of your image, such as "Albums" or "Camera."

❖ **Select Image:** Select the image you want to import and click on it.

❖ **Drag and Drop:** Drag and drop the chosen image onto the timeline at the bottom of the screen.

❖ Alternatively, you can use the "+" button on the timeline and choose "Image" to import images.

It's essential to be aware that CapCut supports a variety of image formats, including JPG, PNG, BMP, and GIF. Additionally, you have the flexibility to adjust settings for your imported images, such as duration and position.

Understanding How To Import Your Own Customize Or Downloaded Stickers In Capcut

To import stickers into CapCut, follow these steps:

❖ **Open CapCut:** Open the CapCut app and start a new project or open an existing one.

❖ **Access Stickers:** Tap on the "Sticker" button located at the bottom of the screen.

❖ **Import Stickers:** Tap on the "Import" button at the top right corner of the sticker library screen, Select the sticker file from your device's storage that you want to import.

❖ **Access Custom Stickers:** Once imported, you can access your custom sticker by tapping on the "Custom" tab in the sticker library.

Note: CapCut supports image files in PNG or JPEG format for importing as stickers.

CHAPTER FIVE

BASIC EDITING TECHNIQUES WITH CAPCUT

Fundamental editing techniques in CapCut encompass importing media, trimming and splitting clips, incorporating text and titles, implementing effects and filters, fine-tuning speed and volume, adjusting clip speed and duration, introducing transitions between clips, and utilizing basic editing tools like crop, rotate, and flip. These methods are employed to craft a refined and professionally styled video, leveraging the diverse tools and features provided by the application. CapCut empowers users to effortlessly edit and elevate their videos, eliminating the necessity for prior editing expertise or costly software.

TRIMMING AND SPLITTING TECHNIQUE

Trimming and splitting clips represent fundamental editing techniques frequently employed to refine and enhance videos. CapCut provides an intuitive and user-friendly interface, simplifying the process for users to trim and split their video clips.

How To Trim A Clip In Capcut

Trimming clips within CapCut facilitates the removal of unwanted or unnecessary segments, ensuring that the video remains concise and visually appealing.

To trim a clip in the CapCut app, follow these steps:

- ❖ Open the CapCut app and select the project you want to work on.
- ❖ Tap on the clip you wish to trim in the timeline at the bottom of the screen.
- ❖ Drag the yellow handles on either side of the clip to adjust the start and end points.
- ❖ Preview the trimmed clip by tapping on the play button.
- ❖ Once satisfied with the trimmed clip, tap on "Save" to save your changes.

It's essential to understand that trimming a clip in CapCut doesn't delete any parts of the original video file; it merely adjusts the start and end points within your project.

How To Split A Clip In Capcut

To split a clip in CapCut, you can follow these steps:

- ❖ Open the CapCut app and select the project you want to edit.
- ❖ Locate the clip you want to split and drag it to the timeline.
- ❖ Move the playhead to the point in the clip where you want to make the split.
- ❖ Click on the "scissors" icon located at the bottom of the screen.
- ❖ Move the playhead to the end of the segment you want to split and click on the "scissors" icon again.
- ❖ Click on the middle segment to select it, then click on the "trash can" icon to delete it.
- ❖ Adjust the remaining segments as desired.

With CapCut, trimming and splitting clips becomes a straightforward and effective way to improve the overall quality of your videos. By utilizing these techniques, you can create visually appealing videos that are bound to captivate your audience.

ADJUSTING CLIP SPEED AND DURATION

In video editing, modifying clip speed and duration is a common practice that provides editors with the ability to manage the tempo of the video and manipulate its overall length. This process entails altering the playback speed of a video clip, achieved by either accelerating or decelerating the clip.

Typically, in video editing software, adjusting clip speed and duration involves selecting the clip on the timeline and accessing its properties. This allows editors to modify the clip's speed by a percentage value or input a specific duration. Slowing down a clip will extend its length, while speeding it up will shorten it.

It's crucial to be aware that changing the speed of a clip can impact its quality and smoothness. Slowing down a clip might result in choppiness or blurriness, while accelerating it may lead to skipped frames or other visual distortions. To address these issues, certain video editing software offers advanced tools for adjusting clip speed and duration, such as frame interpolation and motion blur.

Overall, the ability to adjust clip speed and duration serves as a potent tool for video editors, enabling them to command the rhythm and duration of their videos. By skillfully employing this technique, editors can craft captivating and dynamic content that captures the attention of their audience.

How To Adjust Clip Speed

To adjust the speed of a clip in CapCut, follow these steps:

- ❖ Open the CapCut app and select the project you want to edit.
- ❖ Tap on the clip you wish to adjust the speed for.
- ❖ Select the "Speed" option from the toolbar at the bottom of the screen.
- ❖ Move the slider to the left to slow down the clip or to the right to speed it up.
- ❖ Preview the clip by tapping the play button to see how it looks at the adjusted speed.
- ❖ Once you're satisfied with the speed, tap on the checkmark button to apply the changes.

Additionally, CapCut provides options to reverse a clip or loop it under the "Speed" option, offering opportunities to create unique and visually appealing effects.

How To Adjust Clip Duration

To adjust the duration of a clip in CapCut, follow these steps:

- ❖ Open your project in CapCut and select the clip you want to adjust.
- ❖ Tap on the clip to bring up the editing menu at the bottom of the screen.
- ❖ In the editing menu, you'll see a slider with the current duration of the clip displayed. Slide this left or right to increase or decrease the duration of the clip.
- ❖ You can also manually enter a new duration for the clip by tapping on the duration number and typing in a new value.
- ❖ Once you've adjusted the clip duration to your liking, preview the changes by playing the clip in the preview window.

Adjusting the duration of a clip may impact the overall timing of your project, so make sure to preview your changes to ensure they fit with the rest of your video.

ADDING TRANSITIONS BETWEEN CLIPS WITH CAPCUT

Smoothing the transition between two separate shots in CapCut may be achieved by adding simple transitions between clips.

How To Add Transition Between Clips

Adding transitions between clips in CapCut is a straightforward process that contributes to a seamless transition between two different shots.

Follow these steps to include transitions in your CapCut project:

- ❖ Open your project in CapCut and navigate to the timeline.
- ❖ Select the initial clip to which you want to add a transition.
- ❖ Tap on the "Effects" button at the bottom of the screen.
- ❖ Choose "Transitions" from the menu and select the preferred transition.
- ❖ Drag the chosen transition to the timeline, positioning it between the two clips.
- ❖ Adjust the length of the transition by dragging its edges to make it longer or shorter.
- ❖ Repeat these steps for any additional transitions you wish to include.

For further customization, tap on a transition in the timeline and select "Edit." This will enable you to modify the duration, style, and other settings of the transition.

By incorporating transitions between clips, you enhance the visual flow of your video, making it more polished and engaging. CapCut provides various transition options, such as fades, wipes, and slides, ensuring you can choose transitions that perfectly complement your project.

USING THE BASIC EDITING TOOLS (SUCH AS CROP, ROTATE, AND FLIP)

Capcut offers a selection of fundamental editing tools that you may use to improve the quality of your videos. Among them are the tools for cropping, rotating, and flipping. Here's a more thorough rundown on how to utilize these Capcut tools.

Crop Tool

You may make your clip or videos appear more polished and professional by removing undesired parts with Capcut's crop tool. Just choose the clip you wish to crop and hit the crop symbol to activate this tool. Next, you may use the presets to crop to a given aspect ratio or drag the frame's boundaries to change the crop area.

How to crop with capcut

To crop a video in CapCut, you can follow these steps:

❖ Open CapCut and create a new project or open an existing one.
❖ Import the video you want to crop by tapping on the "+" icon in the media library and selecting the video from your phone's gallery.
❖ Drag the video clip to the timeline at the bottom of the screen.
❖ Tap on the video clip to select it.
❖ Tap on the crop icon, which looks like a square with diagonal lines, in the toolbar at the bottom of the screen.

❖ Drag the edges of the crop frame to adjust the area you want to keep in the video.

❖ Tap on the checkmark icon to apply the crop and save your changes.

By touching on the aspect ratio icon in the toolbar next to the crop button, you may also change the video's aspect ratio. From there, you may manually change the frame by moving its boundaries, or select from a variety of pre-set aspect ratios. You may use CapCut's other tools and capabilities to edit your movie further if you're happy with the crop and aspect ratio.

Rotate Tool

You may rotate your video clip clockwise or counterclockwise with Capcut's rotate tool. Choose the clip you wish to rotate, then hit the rotate symbol to activate this function. After that, you may select the rotation's direction and angle.

How to rotate a clip in CapCut

Here's a step-by-step guide on rotating a clip in CapCut:

❖ **Select the Clip:** Choose the specific clip you intend to rotate from the timeline.

❖ **Access the Transform Tool:** Tap on the "Transform" button, recognizable by a box with an arrow icon.

❖ **Choose Rotate Option:** Select the "Rotate" option within the Transform menu.

❖ **Adjust Rotation:** Utilize the slider to fine-tune the rotation angle as needed. Alternatively, employ your fingers for a manual rotation adjustment.

- ❖ **Confirmation:** Tap on "Done" once content with the rotation effect.
- ❖ **Additional Rotation Options:** Explore further rotation options by tapping on the dedicated buttons for 90-degree clockwise or counterclockwise rotations located next to the slider.

By following these steps, you can easily apply precise rotations to your clips in CapCut, offering creative control over the orientation of your video content.

Flip

You may turn your video clip vertically or horizontally with Capcut's flip feature. Choose the clip you wish to flip, then hit the flip symbol to activate this feature. The flip's direction can then be selected.

In video editing, flipping a video either horizontally or vertically may be a helpful method. Here's how to use CapCut for that:

- ❖ **Open CapCut:** Launch CapCut and either start a new project or open an existing one.
- ❖ **Add Video Clip:** Import the video clip you wish to flip onto the timeline.
- ❖ **Select Clip:** Tap on the specific clip to highlight it, then click the "Effects" button on the toolbar at the bottom.
- ❖ **Access Transform Options:** Scroll down to the "Transform" section within the Effects menu.
- ❖ **Choose Flip:** Under "Transform," select "Flip."
- ❖ **Specify Flip Direction:** Choose between horizontal or vertical flips by tapping the corresponding button.

❖ **For Entire Video:** If you want to flip the entire video clip, select the clip, tap on "Crop" in the toolbar, then hit "Flip." Choose between horizontal or vertical flip.

CapCut goes beyond basic editing tools, offering advanced features like color correction, filters, and special effects. Integrating these advanced tools with the fundamental ones empowers you to craft professional and standout videos.

EFFECT AND FILTER CAPCUT

Effects and filters play a crucial role in elevating the visual appeal of a video during the editing process. CapCut provides users with a diverse array of effects and filters to enhance their videos. Effects are typically employed for introducing special visual enhancements, while filters are utilized to modify the color or tone of a video.

CapCut offers a variety of effects such as glitch, snow, sparkle, and film grain, among others. Filters, on the other hand, encompass options like black and white, vintage, warm, and cool filters.

Incorporating effects and filters into your CapCut project is a straightforward process. Users can select the desired clip, and then tap on the effects or filters icon located at the bottom of the screen. This opens up a selection interface, allowing users to choose from a range of effects or filters to apply to their video.

CapCut further enhances flexibility by enabling users to apply multiple effects and filters to a single clip. This can be achieved by selecting the clip, tapping on the "Effects" icon, and then choosing various effects and filters from different categories.

Beyond effects and filters, CapCut provides additional editing tools such as text overlays, stickers, and music tracks. These tools allow users to incorporate supplementary elements, contributing to an enriched visual and auditory experience in their videos.

How To Add Effects

Follow these steps to add an effect to a clip in CapCut:

- ❖ Launch the CapCut app and open the desired project.
- ❖ Go to the timeline and choose the clip you wish to enhance with an effect.
- ❖ Tap on the "Effects" icon located at the bottom of the screen.
- ❖ Explore the diverse effect categories and pick the one that suits your vision.
- ❖ After selecting the effect, fine-tune the intensity and other parameters as per your preferences.
- ❖ Preview the clip to assess the effect and make any necessary adjustments.
- ❖ Once satisfied, tap on the "Save" button to apply the effect to the clip.

Note that certain effects may not be accessible for free and could require a subscription or payment for full access.

How To Add Filters

To apply a filter to your video in CapCut, follow these steps:

- ❖ Open the video you wish to enhance in the timeline.
- ❖ Tap on the "Filters" option situated on the right side of the screen.

- ❖ Explore the list of available filters and select the one that suits your preferences.
- ❖ Tap on the chosen filter to preview its impact on your video.
- ❖ Once you've made your selection, tap on the checkmark icon to apply the filter to your video.
- ❖ you can fine-tune the filter's strength by adjusting the slider left or right, controlling the intensity of the effect.

Keep in mind that certain filters may not be universally applicable to all videos or clips, and the availability of filters might vary depending on the version of CapCut you are using.

ADDING TEXT AND TITLES IN CAPCUT

Enhancing your videos with text and titles is a powerful way to provide context, highlight key elements, and elevate the overall professionalism of your content. CapCut provides a comprehensive set of tools to facilitate the addition of text and titles to your videos. To incorporate text or titles, initiate the process by selecting the "Text" option from the toolbar positioned at the screen's bottom. Subsequently, you can opt for pre-designed text styles or craft personalized text to suit your preferences.

Customization options abound, allowing you to modify the font, size, color, and alignment of your text. Moreover, you can infuse dynamic and engaging animation effects like sliding or bouncing to enhance its visual appeal. Beyond basic text, CapCut offers an array of title templates designed to infuse stylized titles into your videos. These templates are categorized by themes such as "Travel" or "Fashion" and can be effortlessly tailored to align with your specific requirements.

The process of adding text and titles in CapCut is straightforward yet impactful, serving as an effective means to augment your content and captivate your audience.

How To Add Texts And Titles To Video

To incorporate text and titles in CapCut, follow these straightforward steps:

- ❖ Launch the CapCut app and either create a new project or access an existing one.
- ❖ Tap on the "Text" option located in the bottom menu.
- ❖ Choose the desired text type, such as "Title," "Subtitle," "Caption," or "Credit."
- ❖ From the available options, select the text style that complements your vision.
- ❖ Enter the desired text into the text box and customize aspects like font, size, color, and alignment to your preference.
- ❖ Fine-tune the text duration by adjusting the ends of the text clip on the timeline.
- ❖ Position the text precisely by dragging it to your preferred location on the screen.
- ❖ Add an extra layer of dynamism by incorporating animation effects. Simply navigate to the "Animation" tab and choose from the available options.
- ❖ Once satisfied with the text, tap on the checkmark icon to apply the changes.
- ❖ Repeat these steps if you wish to include additional text or titles in your video.
- ❖ Preview the video, complete with the added text and titles, by tapping the "Play" button.

❖ Finally, export and save your edited video by tapping on the "Export" button.

Incorporating text and titles in CapCut is a swift and efficient method to elevate the quality of your video content.

How To Add Animations To Text

To infuse animation into text and titles within CapCut, adhere to the following steps:

❖ Open CapCut and import the video slated for editing.
❖ Tap on the "Text" icon residing in the toolbar at the bottom of the screen.
❖ Choose the preferred style of text or title for inclusion in your video.
❖ Once text has been inputted, tap on the "Animation" tab positioned at the bottom of the screen.
❖ Select the animation style to be applied to your text or title from the assortment of available options.
❖ Fine-tune the timing and duration of the animation by manipulating the keyframes.
❖ Preview the animation to gauge its appearance within your video.
❖ Upon satisfaction with the animation, tap on the checkmark icon to implement it on your text or title.

It's noteworthy that you possess the flexibility to further tailor the text or title by adjusting parameters such as position, size, font, color, and more. The integration of animation into text and titles can impart a dynamic and captivating quality to your videos. CapCut offers a diverse array of animation styles, encompassing effects like fly-in, fade-in, and zoom-in. Moreover, the platform permits the addition of multiple text and title layers to your video, each endowed with its unique animation and style.

USING STICKERS AND EMOJIS IN VIDEOS

Emojis and stickers are a great way to inject personality and originality into your videos. You can quickly and simply add stickers and emojis to your videos or clips with CapCut in a few easy steps.

You can also include a range of animated emojis and stickers in your film using CapCut. To use an animated sticker or emoji, just choose one from the Sticker Library and add it to your film. As soon as you include the animation in your movie, it will begin to play automatically.

Emojis and stickers may be a creative and entertaining way to add some additional flair to your movies, and using CapCut makes it simple to do so.

How To Add Stickers To Videos In In Capcut

Absolutely! Adding stickers to your videos in CapCut is a breeze. Follow these steps for a seamless experience:

- ❖ **Open CapCut:** Launch the CapCut app on your device.
- ❖ **Create a New Project:** Start a new project or open an existing one.
- ❖ **Import Your Video:** Tap on the "Import" button to bring in the video you want to enhance.
- ❖ **Access Stickers:** Locate and tap on the "Stickers" icon positioned at the bottom of the screen.
- ❖ **Choose a Sticker:** Browse through the diverse collection of stickers available and select the one that suits your video.

- ❖ **Adjust Size and Position:** Drag and resize the chosen sticker to your liking. Position it appropriately on the screen.
- ❖ **Animate the Sticker:** For added flair, tap on the sticker and access the "Animation" options. Choose from various animation styles like "Bounce," "Fade," or "Rotate."
- ❖ **Preview Your Creation:** Play the video in the preview window to see how the sticker animates within your content.
- ❖ **Apply the Sticker:** Once satisfied, tap the checkmark button to confirm and apply the sticker to your video.
- ❖ **Save and Export:** Save your edited masterpiece by tapping the "Export" button. select your preferred video resolution and file format.

With these user-friendly steps, CapCut allows you to effortlessly incorporate stickers into your videos, bringing an extra layer of engagement and fun to your content. Enjoy the creative process!

How To Apply Emoji To Video

Certainly! Adding emojis to your video in CapCut is a straightforward process. Here's a step-by-step guide:

- ❖ **Open CapCut:** Launch the CapCut app on your device.
- ❖ **Start or Open a Project:** Create a new project or open an existing one.
- ❖ **Import Your Video:** Import the video to which you want to add the emoji.
- ❖ **Access Stickers:** Click on the "Sticker" icon located in the bottom toolbar of the app.
- ❖ **Choose Emoji:** From the list of stickers, select the "Emoji" option.

- ❖ **Select Emoji:** Choose the specific emoji you want to include in your video.
- ❖ **Place and Resize:** Drag and drop the chosen emoji onto the desired position in your video. Adjust the size and position using the resizing and positioning tools.
- ❖ **Add Animations:** For an extra touch, click on the "Animation" button in the top toolbar. Select an animation preset to apply dynamic effects to the emoji.
- ❖ **Preview Your Video:** Preview the video to ensure the emoji is well-placed and animated as desired.
- ❖ **Save or Export:** Once satisfied, save or export your video to share it with others.

By following these simple steps, you can seamlessly integrate emojis into your video content, adding a playful and expressive element to enhance viewer engagement. Enjoy creating fun and lively videos with CapCut.

How To Add Animation To Sticker And Emoji

Adding animation to emojis in your video using CapCut is a creative way to make your content more dynamic. Here's a step-by-step guide:

- ❖ **Open CapCut**: Launch the CapCut app and import your video clip into the timeline.
- ❖ **Access Stickers or Emojis:** Go to the "Media" tab and select either "Stickers" or "Emojis."
- ❖ **Choose Sticker or Emoji:** Browse through the available stickers or emojis, or use the search function to find a specific one.
- ❖ **Add to Timeline:** Once you've chosen the sticker or emoji, drag and drop it onto the timeline at the desired position.

- ❖ **Adjust Size and Position:** Use the controls to adjust the size and position of the sticker or emoji according to your preference.
- ❖ **Apply Animation:** Select the sticker or emoji on the timeline. Tap the "Animation" button located on the right side of the screen.
- ❖ **Choose Animation Effect:** From the available options, choose an animation effect that suits your video style.
- ❖ **Adjust Timing and Duration:** Fine-tune the timing and duration of the animation to synchronize it with your video.
- ❖ **Preview Your Video:** Preview your video to ensure that the animated sticker or emoji appears as intended.
- ❖ **Finalize Your Project:** Make any additional adjustments if needed, and finalize your video project.

By following these steps, you can add playful animations to emojis in your videos, enhancing their visual appeal and engagement. Enjoy creating animated and entertaining content with CapCut!

CHAPTER SIX

ADVANCED EDITING TECHNIQUES

using a variety of features and tools, users may create and edit videos using CapCut, an app for video editing. We'll go over a few of the more complex editing methods that may be utilized with CapCut to produce videos of high caliber in this post.

With its array of sophisticated editing techniques, CapCut is a potent video editing program that can assist you in producing films of a high caliber. You may make visually beautiful and captivating videos that will enthrall your audience by using keyframes, text and title addition, transitions, filters, and effects, as well as audio editing capabilities.

UNDERSTANDING KEYFRAMES IN CAPCUT

A key component of video editing that lets you make dynamic, eye-catching videos are keyframes. With the use of keyframes, you may gradually change a video clip's position, rotation, scale, and opacity. Keyframes may be added and modified with ease using CapCut to produce a variety of motion effects, including animations and transitions.

How To Add Keyframes In Capcut

Choose the video clip you wish to edit in CapCut, then press the "Motion" button to add keyframes. This will launch the motion editor, where you may modify the clip's opacity, scale, rotation, and position. Just press the property you wish to change, such as "Position," and then hit the "+" symbol to add a keyframe at the current time marker.

How To Adjust Keyframes In Capcut

After adding a keyframe, you may move it across the timeline to change its attributes. By choosing the keyframe and moving the controls on the screen, you may also change its characteristics. To generate a seamless rotation effect, for instance, you may add a keyframe for the rotation property and then change the keyframe's angle.

How To Use Keyframes To Animate Effects

Utilizing keyframes for animating effects is a potent method to introduce movement and enhance the visual appeal of your videos. Here's a guide on employing keyframes to animate effects in CapCut.

- ❖ Begin by selecting the effect you wish to animate. CapCut provides a diverse array of effects, including color correction, filters, and stickers, all applicable to your video clips. Once you've chosen the effect, apply it to your video clip.
- ❖ Proceed to add keyframes to the effect slated for animation. Select the video clip housing the effect, then tap the "Motion" button to access the motion editor. Within the editor, choose the effect you want to animate, like "Saturation," and tap the "+" icon to insert a keyframe at the current time marker.
- ❖ Once keyframes are in place, fine-tune their properties to craft the desired animation. For instance, if you aim to gradually increase the saturation, place a keyframe at the clip's start with a lower saturation value and another at the end with a higher saturation value.
- ❖ Further, customize the animation by adjusting keyframe properties such as timing and easing. Timing pertains to the animation's duration while easing relates to its acceleration and

deceleration. Tweaking these aspects results in a smoother, more natural animation.

❖ Preview the animation to assess its appearance within the video clip. Refine the animation by adjusting keyframe properties or incorporating additional keyframes if needed.

❖ Should you wish to apply the same animation effect to other video clips, copy and paste the effect keyframes. Select the clip with the desired keyframes, tap "Copy," then choose the target clip and tap "Paste" to transfer the keyframes.

By adhering to these steps, you can leverage keyframes effectively in CapCut to animate effects, culminating in dynamic and visually captivating videos.

How To Use Keyframes To Create Motion Effects

Utilizing keyframes in CapCut opens up possibilities for generating diverse motion effects. For instance, keyframes offer the capability to craft animations, like moving text or graphics, through the dynamic adjustment of element positions and scales over a specific duration. Additionally, keyframes can be instrumental in the creation of transitions, including fades, dissolves, and wipes, achieved by manipulating the opacity and position of the video clips throughout the sequence.

To create motion using keyframes in CapCut, follow these steps:

❖ **Choose Your Effect:** Begin by selecting the video clip or element to which you want to apply motion. CapCut offers various effects, such as text, graphics, or video clips.

- ❖ **Apply the Effect:** Apply the chosen effect to your video clip or element. For example, you might want to add text or a sticker to your video.

- ❖ **Access the Motion Editor:** Once the effect is applied, tap on the clip or element to select it. Look for the "Motion" option and tap on it to open the motion editor.

- ❖ **Add Keyframes:** Within the motion editor, identify the parameters you want to animate, such as position, scale, opacity, etc. Tap the "+" icon to add keyframes at specific points in the timeline.

- ❖ **Adjust Keyframe Properties:** After adding keyframes, move to each keyframe and adjust the properties accordingly. For example, if you're animating text, you can set keyframes to change its position or scale over time. If you're creating a transition, adjust opacity or position keyframes.

- ❖ **Fine-Tune Timing and Easing:** To enhance the motion's fluidity, adjust the timing and easing of the keyframes. This step ensures a smooth and natural progression of the effect.

- ❖ **Preview Your Animation:** Play the timeline to preview how your motion effect looks. Make adjustments as needed, going back to the motion editor if further refinement is necessary.

- ❖ **Copy and Paste Keyframes (Optional):** If you want to apply the same motion to other elements or clips, use the copy and paste functions in the motion editor. This saves time and maintains consistency across your project.

- ❖ **Review and Finalize:** Carefully review your entire video to ensure the motion effects align with your creative vision. Make any final adjustments to achieve the desired outcome.

- ❖ **Export Your Video:** Once satisfied with your motion effects, export your video to save or share it.

By following these steps, you can effectively use keyframes to create engaging motion effects in CapCut, adding dynamic elements to your videos.

UNDERSTANDING COLOR AND EXPOSURE

Color and exposure play pivotal roles in video editing, significantly influencing the overall aesthetics of your video content. Within CapCut, you have access to numerous tools and features designed to modify the color and exposure settings of your video clips. Here is a summary of how you can manipulate color and exposure in CapCut:

How To Add Color And Exposure

Incorporating color and exposure enhancements into your video clips within CapCut is a simple and intuitive process. Follow these steps to achieve the desired adjustments.

❖ Begin by launching CapCut and importing the video clip you intend to modify for color and exposure. Initiate this by tapping the "+" button on the app's main screen, followed by the selection of your desired video clip from your phone's media library.

❖ Once your video clip is imported, tap on it to access the editing tools. Within this interface, the "Edit" button will open up options for color and exposure adjustments.

❖ To fine-tune the color and exposure of your video clip, select either the "Color" or "Exposure" buttons in the editing tools. Utilize the sliders or presets to make adjustments to properties such as brightness, contrast, saturation, hue, and temperature.

❖ After implementing your adjustments, preview the video clip to evaluate the visual impact of the changes. If needed, return to the color and exposure tools to make further refinements.

❖ If you wish to apply identical color and exposure adjustments across multiple video clips, utilize the copy-and-paste function. Simply tap the "Copy" button associated with the adjustments you want to replicate, select the target video clips, and then tap "Paste" to seamlessly apply the adjustments to the chosen clips.

How To Adjust Color In Capcut

❖ To modify the color of your video clips, start by selecting the clip you wish to alter and then tap on the "Edit" button. Subsequently, access the color correction tool by tapping on the "Color" button.

❖ Within the color correction tool, you have the flexibility to adjust various color properties such as brightness, contrast, saturation, hue, and temperature. These adjustments can be made using sliders for precision, or you can employ presets by tapping on the corresponding icons. Additionally, the eyedropper tool enables you to select a color from one part of the video clip and apply it to another section.

❖ Once you've completed your color adjustments, preview the clip to assess the visual impact. If necessary, revisit the color correction tool to make further refinements and modifications as needed.

How To Adjust Exposure In Capcut

❖ To modify the exposure of your video clips, start by selecting the clip you wish to adjust and then tap on the "Edit" button.

Subsequently, open the exposure tool by tapping on the "Exposure" button.

❖ Within the exposure tool, you can adjust various exposure properties, including brightness, contrast, highlights, and shadows. These adjustments can be made using sliders for precision, or you can tap on the icons to apply presets.

❖ Once you've completed your exposure adjustments, preview the clip to evaluate the visual impact. If necessary, revisit the exposure tool to make additional refinements and modifications.

CapCut also provides several advanced color and exposure adjustment tools that enable further refinement of your video clips. These tools include:

❖ **Curve Tool:** Adjusts the color and brightness of specific tonal ranges in your video clip.

❖ **HSL Tool:** Enables adjustment of the hue, saturation, and luminance of specific colors in your video clip.

❖ **Color Wheel Tool:** Allows adjustment of the color balance and temperature of your video clip.

By incorporating these advanced tools alongside the basic color and exposure adjustment tools, you can craft visually stunning videos with vibrant colors and impeccable exposure.

UNDERSTANDING MASKING AND BLENDING MODE

Using CapCut's advanced editing capabilities, such as the masking and blending modes, you may produce visually spectacular videos. This is a summary of how to utilize CapCut's blending and masking modes:

Masking

You may use the masking technique to reveal or conceal specific areas of a video clip. Masks in CapCut may be used to produce special effects, such as hiding components or making items vanish.

How To Mask In Capcut

❖ **Initiating Mask Creation:** To commence crafting a mask, the first step involves incorporating a mask layer onto your chosen video clip. Begin by selecting the target video clip, then tap the "Layer" button. Subsequently, opt for "Mask" to introduce a mask layer atop the video clip.

❖ **Choosing Mask Shape:** Following the addition of the mask layer, determine the shape of the mask by tapping the "Mask Shape" button. A range of options, including rectangle, ellipse, and freehand, allows you to select the most suitable shape for your masking needs.

❖ **Adjusting Mask Properties:** After settling on the mask shape, fine-tune its properties by tapping the "Mask" button. Within this interface, you gain the ability to refine the mask's position, size, feather, and opacity according to your desired specifications.

❖ **Previewing Initial Adjustments:** Upon completing the preliminary adjustments, assess the appearance of the mask by previewing the video clip. If necessary, refine the mask further by returning to the mask properties and implementing additional modifications.

By following these steps, you can seamlessly create and customize masks within your CapCut editing process, enhancing the visual elements of your video content.

Blending Modes

Blending modes serve as a technique to merge two or more video clips, resulting in distinctive visual effects. Within CapCut, an array of blending modes is available, each imparting a distinct effect to the composite video.

How To Add Blending Mode To A Layer

❖ **Initiating Blending Mode Effect:** To commence crafting a blending mode effect, the initial step involves introducing a layer atop the designated video clip. Select the video clip, then tap the "Layer" button, followed by choosing "Add Layer" to incorporate a new layer.

❖ **Selecting Blending Mode:** After adding the new layer, determine the blending mode by tapping the "Blending" button. Within this menu, an assortment of blending modes, such as multiply, screen, overlay, and more, awaits your selection.

❖ **Adjusting Layer Opacity:** Following the choice of the blending mode, regulate the effect's intensity by adjusting the layer's opacity. This can be achieved by tapping the "Opacity" button and manipulating the slider to attain the desired strength.

❖ **Previewing Initial Adjustments:** After completing the preliminary adjustments, evaluate the appearance of the blending mode by previewing the video clip. Should the need arise, refine the blending mode further by revisiting the blending mode properties and implementing additional modifications.

By employing masking and blending modes within CapCut, you gain the capability to generate distinctive and visually striking video effects, setting your videos apart with creative flair.

UNDERSTANDING SOUND EFFECTS

Enhancing your video with sound effects can elevate its overall quality and captivate your audience. CapCut offers diverse sound effect options, enabling you to incorporate unique and creative audio elements into your video. Here's a guide on how to add sound effects in CapCut:

How To Add Sound Effects In Capcut

❖ **Open CapCut and Import Media:** Launch CapCut and initiate the process by importing the desired video and audio clips. Tap the "Import" button located at the bottom of the screen, and select the video and audio files you intend to use.

❖ **Arrange Audio on the Timeline:** Once your video and audio clips are imported, drag the audio clip onto the timeline beneath the video clip. Tap the audio clip to access the "Audio" panel, and then select the "Sound Effects" button to explore the sound effect library.

❖ **Explore Sound Effect Categories:** Within the sound effect library, you'll find various categories such as animal sounds, transportation sounds, and more. Choose the relevant category and browse through the available sound effects. To preview a sound effect, simply tap on it.

❖ **Adjust Sound Effect Settings:** Upon selecting a sound effect, customize its settings to suit your video. Modify the volume by dragging the volume slider, and refine the start and end points of the sound effect by manipulating the waveform.

❖ **Preview and Adjust:** After making the necessary adjustments, preview your video to ensure the synchronization of the sound effects with your content. Once satisfied with the result, proceed to export your video by tapping on the "Export" button located at the top right corner of the screen.

CHAPTER SEVEN

EXPORTING VIDEOS IN CAPCUT

Concluding your video project in CapCut involves the crucial step of exporting, and determining the quality and format of your final output. Follow this comprehensive guide on the exporting process in CapCut:

❖ Ensure Completion of Editing: Before initiating the export, verify that your video editing is complete. Confirm the placement of transitions, effects, and audio elements, ensuring satisfaction with the final product.

❖ Tap the "Export" Button: When ready to export, tap the "Export" button positioned at the top right corner of the screen. This action prompts the export settings menu, allowing adjustments to the output resolution, format, and other parameters.

- **Resolution:** CapCut offers a spectrum of resolution options, ranging from 360p to 1080p and even 4K.
- **Format:** Choose from various export formats, including MP4, MOV, and GIF.
- **Quality:** Adjust video quality by selecting the "Quality" option. Higher quality settings result in larger file sizes, while lower settings yield smaller files.
- **Export Speed:** Tailor the export speed to influence processing time. Higher speeds mean faster exports with potential quality trade-offs, while lower speeds prioritize quality with extended export times.

❖ **Initiate Export Process:** After setting the desired export parameters, tap the "Export" button at the bottom of the screen.

Depending on your video's length and complexity, the export process may take time. Monitor progress by tapping the "Export" button again.

❖ **Save or Share Your Video**: Upon completion of the export, save your video to your device's storage or share it directly on social media platforms. To save, tap the "Save" button at the screen's bottom, choose your desired location, and confirm the action.

Exporting your video in CapCut involves selecting appropriate export settings and tapping the "Export" button. Opt for the right resolution, format, and quality to ensure optimal output for your video project.

CHAPTER EIGHT

OTHER BASIC EDITING OPERATIONS

HOW TO MAKE YOUR PHOTO BECOME CARTOON IN CAPCUT

- ❖ **Ensure the CapCut Application is Updated:** Confirm that your smartphone has the latest version of the CapCut application installed.
- ❖ **Launch the CapCut Application and Create a New Project:** Open the CapCut application and initiate a new project.
- ❖ **Add the Desired Photo for Cartoon Editing:** Incorporate the photo you wish to transform into a cartoon.
- ❖ **Access the Editing Menu:** After adding the photo, either click on the Edit menu or tap the photo layer on the timeline.
- ❖ **Navigate to the Anime Filter Menu:** Locate and open the menu containing various anime filters.
- ❖ **Select an Anime Style or Filter:** Choose from a range of anime styles or filters, including cartoons, comics, sketches, or anime itself. For this demonstration, let's select the cartoon style.
- ❖ **Wait for the Generation Process to Complete:** Allow the generation process to reach 100% completion.
- ❖ **Successful Cartoon Transformation:** Your photo has now been successfully transformed into a cartoon.
- ❖ **Save the Cartoon Photo:** To save your cartoon version, tap the full-screen icon situated in the top right corner.

❖ **Capture a Screenshot on Your Smartphone:** Capture a screenshot on your smartphone, ensuring that your cartoon photo is successfully saved to your gallery.

HOW TO MAKE YOUR PHOTO BECOME ANIME IN CAPCUT

❖ **Ensure Your CapCut Application is Up-to-Date:** Confirm that your smartphone has the latest version of the CapCut application installed.

❖ **Launch the CapCut Application and Start a New Project:** Open the CapCut application and initiate the creation of a new project.

❖ **Incorporate the Desired Photo for Anime Editing:** Add the photo you intend to edit into an anime style.

❖ **Access the Editing Menu:** After adding the photo, either click on the Edit menu or tap the photo layer on the timeline.

❖ **Navigate to the Anime Filter Menu:** Find and open the menu housing various anime filters.

❖ **Select an Anime Style or Filter:** Choose from a variety of anime styles or filters, such as cartoons, comics, sketches, or anime itself. For this instance, opt for the anime style.

❖ **Wait for the Generation Process to Complete:** Allow the generation process to reach completion, ensuring it reaches 100%.

❖ **Successful Transformation into Anime:** Your photo has now successfully transformed into an anime style.

❖ **Save Your Anime Photo:** To save your anime version, tap the full-screen icon located in the top right corner.

❖ **Capture a Screenshot on Your Smartphone:** Capture a screenshot on your smartphone to ensure that your anime photo is successfully saved to your gallery.

HOW TO CHANGE YOUR PHOTO INTO COMICS IN CAPCUT

❖ **Ensure the Latest Version of CapCut is Installed on Your Smartphone:** Verify that your smartphone has the most recent version of the CapCut application installed.

❖ **Launch the CapCut Application and Initiate a New Project:** Open the CapCut application and start a new project.

❖ **Incorporate the Desired Photo for Comics Editing:** Add the photo you wish to edit into a comic style.

❖ **Access the Editing Menu:** After adding the photo, either click on the Edit menu or tap the photo layer on the timeline.

❖ **Navigate to the Anime Filter Menu:** Find and open the menu featuring various anime filters.

❖ **Select a Comics Style or Filter:** Choose from the available anime styles or filters, which include cartoons, comics, sketches, and anime itself. For this purpose, select the comic style.

❖ **Wait for the Generation Process to Reach 100%:** Allow the generation process to reach completion, ensuring it reaches 100%.

❖ **Successful Transformation into Comics:** Your photo has now been successfully transformed into a comic style.

❖ **Save Your Comics Photo:** To save your comics version, tap the fullscreen icon positioned in the top right corner.

❖ **Capture a Screenshot on Your Smartphone:** Capture a screenshot on your smartphone to ensure that your comic version is successfully saved to your gallery.

HOW TO CHANGE YOUR PHOTO INTO SKETCH IN CAPCUT

❖ **Ensure the Latest Version of CapCut is Installed on Your Smartphone:** Verify that your smartphone has the most recent version of the CapCut application installed.

❖ **Launch the CapCut Application and Start a New Project:** Open the CapCut application and initiate the creation of a new project.

❖ **Add the Desired Photo for Sketch Editing:** Incorporate the photo you wish to edit into a sketch style.

❖ **Access the Editing Menu:** After adding the photo, either click on the Edit menu or tap the photo layer on the timeline.

❖ **Navigate to the Anime Filter Menu:** Find and open the menu containing various anime filters.

❖ **Select a Sketch Style or Filter:** Choose from the available anime styles or filters, including cartoons, comics, sketches, and anime itself. Opt for the sketch style for this demonstration.

❖ **Wait for the Generation Process to Reach 100%:** Allow the generation process to reach completion, ensuring it reaches 100%.

❖ **Successful Transformation into Sketch:** Your photo has now been successfully transformed into a sketch style.

❖ **Save Your Sketch Photo:** To save your sketch version, tap the fullscreen icon situated in the top right corner.

- ❖ **Capture a Screenshot on Your Smartphone:** Capture a screenshot on your smartphone to ensure that your sketch version is successfully saved to your gallery.

Please note that the CapCut application does not have a direct image-saving feature. If you attempt to save your anime, comics, cartoon, and sketch photos using the export option, your photos will be saved in .MP4 video format instead of image format.

HOW TO ADD BACKGROUND MUSIC TO A VIDEO

CapCut stands out as a widely used video editing application that empowers users to incorporate background music into their videos effortlessly. Here's a step-by-step guide to achieving this:

- ❖ **Launch CapCut and Choose Your Video:** Open the CapCut app and select the video you wish to edit.
- ❖ **Access the Music/Audio Menu:** Tap on the "Music" or "Audio" button situated at the bottom of the screen.
- ❖ **Navigate to the Sounds Options:** Click or tap on the "Sounds" option within the menu.
- ❖ **Explore and Choose Music Tracks:** A variety of music tracks will be presented. Explore different genres or utilize the search bar to locate a specific track.
- ❖ **Select and Preview the Chosen Track:** Once you've chosen a track, tap on it to preview it. Adjust the volume of the track using the provided slider if needed.
- ❖ **Incorporate Your Music:** If you prefer to add your music, tap on "My Music" and select a song from your device's music library.

- ❖ **Drag and Drop the Music onto the Timeline:** To integrate the chosen music, simply drag and drop the music track onto the timeline.
- ❖ **Trim the Music Track to Fit the Video Length:** Trim the music track by dragging its edges to align with the length of your video.
- ❖ **Adjust Music Volume:** Fine-tune the volume of the music track by tapping on the audio icon and utilizing the slider.

Following these steps ensures the successful incorporation of background music into your video using CapCut.

HOW TO EXTRACT AUDIO FROM VIDEO IN CAPCUT

- ❖ To extract audio in CapCut, follow these steps:
- ❖ Launch the CapCut application on your mobile device.
- ❖ Select the desired video clip for audio extraction.
- ❖ Tap on the clip to access the editing menu.
- ❖ Navigate to the "Audio" icon located at the bottom of the screen.
- ❖ Select "Extract audio" from the menu.
- ❖ Choose a destination to save the extracted audio file.
- ❖ Tap "Export" to save the audio file.

It's essential to be aware that not all video clips in CapCut support audio extraction. If the "Extract" option is not visible under the "Audio" menu, it indicates that audio extraction is not available for that specific clip.

HOW TO ADD VOICEOVER TO A VIDEO

❖ Launch the CapCut app and choose the video where you wish to include a voiceover.

❖ Access the audio menu.

❖ Select the "Voiceover" option by tapping on it.

❖ Initiate recording by pressing and holding the recorder key.

❖ Grant permission for CapCut to record audio when prompted; click on the "Allow" option.

❖ Speak into the microphone while holding down the recording button. Release the button once you have finished recording.

❖ Finally, tap the checkmark button to proceed to the editing phase.

HOW TO REMOVE BACKGROUND WITHOUT GREENSCREEN

Before proceeding with the background removal process in the video using CapCut, ensure that you have updated the CapCut app on your Android smartphone to the latest version. The feature we will utilize for removing video backgrounds without green screens is part of the latest update, and it won't be available in older versions of the CapCut app.

Here's a step-by-step guide:

❖ **Update CapCut App:** Ensure you have the latest version of the CapCut app installed on your Android smartphone.

❖ **Open CapCut and Create a New Project:** Launch the latest version of the CapCut application and initiate a new project.

- ❖ **Add Video or Photo to Replace Background:** Incorporate a video or photo that will serve as the replacement background in CapCut.
- ❖ **Access the Overlay Menu:** Open the Overlay menu located at the bottom of the screen and tap on "Add overlay."
- ❖ **Add Video for Background Removal:** Integrate a video whose background you intend to remove.
- ❖ **Navigate to the Remove Background Menu:** After adding the video, find and tap on the "Remove background" option at the bottom.
- ❖ **Wait for Background Removal Process:** Allow the background removal process to proceed until it reaches 100%.
- ❖ **Completion of Background Removal:** The process of removing the video background without using a green screen is now complete in CapCut.

By following these steps, you can effectively remove the background from a video using CapCut's latest feature.

HOW TO ADD BACKGROUND WITH GREEN GREENSCREEN

A green screen is a background in videos typically of a single color, often green, although other colors like red, blue, black, or white are also used. If you're using the CapCut video editing software, here's a guide on changing the video background with a green screen:

- ❖ **Launch the CapCut App:** Open the CapCut app installed on your Android smartphone and start a new project.
- ❖ **Add Background Video or Image:** Incorporate a background, either in the form of a video or an image, to be added to the

main video. For instance, let's explore how to add a background image to a video on Android.

- ❖ **Access the Overlay Menu:** Open the Overlay menu located at the bottom of the screen.
- ❖ **Add Overlay:** Tap "Add overlay" to introduce the green screen video that you intend to remove the background from.
- ❖ **Navigate to the Chroma Key Menu:** Find and open the Chroma Key menu at the bottom of the screen.
- ❖ **Select the Background Color:** In the Color Picker menu, choose a green color or any background color that you wish to replace with the previously added background image.
- ❖ **Adjust Intensity:** On the Intensity menu, adjust the slider until the selected green color disappears. It doesn't need to be 100%, just enough to make the background color invisible.
- ❖ **Add Shadows (Optional):** If desired, on the Shadow menu, you can apply shadows to create a more blended effect with the replacement background.
- ❖ **Apply Chroma Key Effect:** Tap the check mark to apply the Chroma Key Effect.

With these steps, you have successfully added a background to your video using the green screen feature in the CapCut app.

HOW TO ADD BACKGROUND WITHOUT GREENSCREEN

Videos with diverse backgrounds, showcasing nature, forests, beaches, shopping centers, and more, often present a variety of colors. If you're using the CapCut application, here's a guide on changing the background in a video without the need for a green screen:

- ❖ **Initiate a New Project:** Start a new project from the home screen of the CapCut app.
- ❖ **Incorporate Replacement Background:** Add a video or image that you want to use as the replacement background.
- ❖ **Access the Overlay Menu:** Open the Overlay menu at the bottom and tap "Add overlay."
- ❖ **Integrate Videos with Regular Backgrounds:** Add videos with diverse backgrounds or videos that do not have green screen backgrounds.
- ❖ **Navigate to the Remove Background Menu:** Find and tap on the "Remove background" option at the bottom.
- ❖ **Await the Background Removal Process**: Allow the process of removing the video background without a green screen to complete.

The process of adding a background to a video without the use of a green screen is now complete using the CapCut application.

HOW TO DO WHITE FLASH IN CAPCUT

In a previous article, I covered CapCut transition effects, specifically discussing how to transition in CapCut. If you've already gone through that article, understanding how to create a white flash on CapCut will be straightforward. However, if you haven't, here's a step-by-step guide for you to learn and practice:

- ❖ **Open CapCut and Start a New Project:** Launch your CapCut app and either tap to open an existing project or create a new one.
- ❖ **Add Two Videos, Photos, or Both:** Integrate two videos, two photos, or a combination of both into your project.
- ❖ **Access the CapCut Transition Menu:** Tap on the CapCut transition button or navigate to the menu in the frame where the two videos meet.
- ❖ **Select Basic Transition:** Ensure you have chosen and are in the Basic Transition section.
- ❖ **Choose the White Flash CapCut Effect:** Locate the White Flash CapCut effect and tap to select it.
- ❖ **Adjust Duration of the White Flash Effect:** Set the duration for which you want the white flash effect to last.
- ❖ **Apply the White Flash Effect:** Finally, tap the checkmark button to apply the white flash effect.

It's worth noting that the white flash effect tends to work exceptionally well when used with slow-motion videos, creating an aesthetically pleasing visual impact.

HOW TO MAKE A VELOCITY EDIT ON CAPCUT

It's essential to understand how to perform velocity edits on CapCut, and the following is a fundamental tutorial. For more advanced techniques, feel free to unleash your creativity and explore further possibilities.

❖ **Launch CapCut on Your Android Device and Start a New Project:** Open the CapCut application on your Android device and initiate a new project.

❖ **Add the Video for Velocity Editing:** Integrate the video that you intend to edit using the velocity technique.

❖ **Incorporate Music or Songs:** If desired, add music to your project. Refer to the tutorial on how to add music in CapCut for guidance.

❖ **Access the Edit Menu:** Open the Edit menu located at the bottom of the screen or tap the video layer on the timeline.

❖ **Navigate to the Speed Menu:** Tap and open the Speed menu.

❖ **Choose the Curve Option for Velocity Edits:** To perform velocity edits, select the Curve option to adjust the speed of the video.

❖ **Select the Custom Curve Option:** Opt for the Custom Curve option, allowing you to personally adjust the video speed.

❖ **Tap Edit After Selecting a Custom Curve:** Proceed to tap Edit after choosing a custom curve.

❖ **Adjust Speed Using Beats:** You'll encounter 5 beats to edit the video speed.

❖ **Increase or Decrease Speed Using Beat Points:** Slide one of the beat points upward to accelerate the video. Conversely, slide a beat point downward to decelerate the video. For instance, increase the second beat point to make it 9.9x faster, and decrease the fourth beat point to be 0.1x slower.

❖ **Apply Velocity Video Effects:** Tap the checkmark button to apply velocity video effects and techniques.

Feel free to experiment with these steps and discover unique and captivating velocity edits for your videos!

HOW TO SHAKE THE SCREEN ON CAPCUT

- ❖ **Initiate a New Project on the Latest Version of the CapCut App:** Start a new project directly from the home screen of the most recent version of the CapCut app.
- ❖ **Incorporate a Photo or Video Intended for the Shaking Effect:** Add a photo or video to the project that you want to enhance with the shaking effect in CapCut.
- ❖ **Access the Effects Menu at the Bottom:** Locate and open the Effects menu positioned at the bottom of the screen.
- ❖ **Navigate to the Basic Effect Category:** Tap on the Basic Effect category within the Effects menu.
- ❖ **Select the "Shake" Effect:** Look for an effect named "Shake" and choose it.
- ❖ **Apply the CapCut Shaking Effect:** Tap the checkmark button to apply the shaking effect in CapCut.
- ❖ **Adjust the Duration of the Added Shake Effect:** Finally, customize the duration of the applied shake effect according to your preferences.

These simple steps will enable you to incorporate the shaking effect seamlessly into your photo or video using CapCut.

HOW TO IMPORT GIFS INTO CAPCUT

To incorporate a GIF directly into CapCut without the need for prior conversion to a video, add it as a sticker instead of an overlay. Follow these step-by-step instructions:

- ❖ **Start a New Project from the CapCut Application Home Screen:** Begin by creating a new project directly from the home screen of the CapCut application.

- ❖ **Include a Photo or Video for GIF Integration:** Add a photo or video to which you intend to attach GIFs.
- ❖ **Access the Stickers Menu at the Bottom:** Open the Stickers menu located at the bottom of the screen.
- ❖ **Tap the Add Sticker Button to Import GIFs:** Use the Add Sticker button to import GIFs directly from your gallery.
- ❖ **Select and Tap the Desired GIF Image:** Browse through your gallery, select the GIF image you wish to add to your video and tap on it.
- ❖ **Tap the Checkmark Button:** Finalize the process by tapping the checkmark button, completing the addition of GIFs to your CapCut project.

Following these steps allows you to seamlessly integrate GIFs into your project in CapCut without the need to convert them to a video format first.

HOW TO MAKE A GIF MOVE IN CAPCUT

- ❖ **Initiate the GIFs Frame:** Commence by tapping the "add keyframe" button at the beginning of the GIFs frame. Subsequently, drag the GIF image to the far left of the video.
- ❖ **Conclude the GIFs Frame:** Move to the end of the GIFs frame and tap the "add keyframe" button. Proceed to drag the GIF image to the far right of the video.
- ❖ **Review the GIF Image Movement:** To observe the results of the GIF image's movement, simply tap the play button.

By following these steps, you can create a dynamic movement for your GIFs within the video frame, enhancing the visual appeal of your project in CapCut.

HOW TO TWEEN ON CAPCUT TO MAKE YOUR GACHA CHARACTER WALK

To animate a Gacha Life character using a GIF image in CapCut, specifically creating a walking animation through the tweening technique, follow these step-by-step instructions:

- ❖ **Initiate a New Project:** Begin by tapping and creating a new project within the CapCut app.
- ❖ **Add a Background for Your Gacha Character:** Integrate a background for your Gacha character, whether it's a video or an image.
- ❖ **Access the Stickers Menu:** Open the Stickers menu located at the bottom of the screen.
- ❖ **Add GIFs to CapCut:** Tap the plus sticker icon to add GIFs to CapCut.
- ❖ **Import Your Gacha Character's Animated GIFs:** Locate and import the animated GIFs of your Gacha character.
- ❖ **Apply Keyframes for Tweening:** At the beginning of the Gacha frame, tap the "Add keyframe" button. Subsequently, drag your Gacha character to the initial position for movement. At the end of the Gacha frame, tap the "Add keyframe" button again. Now, move your Gacha character to the final position where it will stop moving.
- ❖ **Preview the Animation:** Finally, tap the play button to preview the animation and see your Gacha character appear to be walking.

By diligently following these steps, you can achieve a captivating walking animation for your Gacha Life character using the tweening technique in CapCut.

HOW TO USE THE 3D ZOOM EFFECT IN THE CAPCUT APP

To add a 3D zoom effect in CapCut, follow these step-by-step instructions, located in the same menu as the anime and cartoon effects discussed in a previous article on turning photos into anime in CapCut.

❖ **Open the Latest Version of CapCut:** Launch the latest version of the CapCut application and initiate a new project.

❖ **Add Photos for 3D Zoom Effect:** Import one or more photos simultaneously that you intend to enhance with a 3D zoom effect.

❖ **Access the Edit Menu:** Open the Edit menu by tapping on the photo layer within the timeline.

❖ **Navigate to the Style Menu:** Locate and open the Style menu, where various styles can be applied to your photo.

❖ **Choose the 3D Zoom Style:** Within the Style menu, several options will be displayed. Select and tap the 3D Zoom style.

❖ **Wait for 3D Zoom Effect Processing:** Allow the application to process and create the 3D zoom effect. Be patient during this step.

❖ **Apply the 3D Zoom Effect:** Finally, tap the check button to apply the 3D zoom effect in CapCut. To see the result, tap the play button.

By following these steps, you can seamlessly incorporate a captivating 3D zoom effect into your photos using CapCut.

HOW TO CLONE YOURSELF IN A VIDEO USING CAPCUT

Creating a clone effect in CapCut without a green screen involves merging two videos onto the same screen and using the Split mask feature to display both images simultaneously. Follow this comprehensive tutorial for step-by-step guidance:

❖ **Initiate a New Project:** Start a new project within the CapCut app.

❖ **Add Videos with a Common Background**: Import all videos that share the same background into the project.

❖ **Access the Overlay Menu:** Open the Overlay menu located at the bottom of the screen.

❖ **Set the Second Video as an Overlay:** Make the second video an overlay by tapping the second video layer in the timeline and accessing the second Overlay menu.

❖ **Position the Second Video Layer:** Drag and drop the second video layer, used as an overlay, parallel to the position of the first video layer.

❖ **Open the Mask Menu:** While the second video layer is active, find and open the Mask menu at the bottom.

❖ **Select the CapCut Split Mask:** Choose the CapCut Split mask option from the menu.

❖ **Adjust the Split Line:** Rotate the split line until the images in both videos are visible on the screen.

❖ **Apply the Split Mask:** Finally, tap the checkmark button to apply the Split mask and complete the clone effect.

By following these steps, you can achieve a convincing clone effect on CapCut without the need for a green screen.

HOW TO REVERSE A VIDEO ON CAPCUT

Before learning how to play a video in reverse on your Android device, ensure that you have the latest version of the CapCut application installed. If you haven't done so, download and install it for free from the Google Play Store. Follow these steps to reverse a video using CapCut.

- ❖ **Launch the CapCut App:** Open the CapCut application on your Android device and start a New project.
- ❖ **Add the Video:** Select and add the video that you wish to play in reverse.
- ❖ **Access the Edit Menu:** Open the Edit menu or tap on the video clip within the timeline.
- ❖ **Navigate to Reverse Option:** Locate the Reverse menu within the options and tap on it.
- ❖ **Wait for the Reversing Process:** Allow a few seconds for the video reversing process to complete.
- ❖ **Success:** Your video has now been successfully played in reverse.

By following these steps, you can effortlessly play a video in reverse using the CapCut application on your Android device.

HOW TO REVERSE AUDIO OR SOUND ON CAPCUT

To reverse audio in CapCut, you need to convert the desired audio, whether it's music or a song, into a video with the .mp4 format. Once done, you can use the CapCut Reverse menu, as explained in my previous article on reversing videos on Android. Here's the step-by-step tutorial:

- ❖ **Create a New Project:** Begin by creating a new project in the CapCut application.
- ❖ **Add a Photo or Image:** Include any photo or image in the project.
- ❖ **Add the Music or Song:** Insert the music or song you want to reverse using the Audio menu.
- ❖ **Save the Video with Music:** Save the video with the added music to the gallery in .mp4 format.
- ❖ **Create a New Project Again:** Initiate a new project and add the video containing the reversed audio.
- ❖ **Access the Edit Menu:** Open the Edit menu at the bottom or tap the video clip on the timeline.
- ❖ **Navigate to Reverse Option:** Find the Reverse menu and tap on it.
- ❖ **Wait for the Reversing Process:** Allow a few seconds for the video and audio reversing the process to complete.
- ❖ **Separate the Reversed Audio:** Optionally, you can separate the reversed audio from the video using the Extract Audio menu.
- ❖ **Preview the Results:** Tap the play button to listen to the reversed audio and see the results.

Following these steps will guide you through the process of reversing audio in CapCut, providing you with the desired reversed audio effect.

HOW TO FLIP VIDEO HORIZONTALLY USING CAPCUT

Flipping or mirroring a video on Android using the CapCut video editor app is a straightforward process. With just a simple click, your selfie video can be instantly reversed according to your preference. To experience it yourself, follow these easy steps:

❖ **Open CapCut:** Launch the CapCut app after installing it and start a new project.

❖ **Add Your Selfie Video:** Choose and add the selfie video you want to flip.

❖ **Access the Edit Menu:** Open the Edit menu or tap on the video clip within the timeline.

❖ **Navigate to the Second Edit Menu:** Locate and tap on the second Edit menu.

❖ **Select the Mirror Option:** Choose and tap the Mirror option. Your selfie video will be instantly flipped.

❖ **Save the Flipped Video:** Finally, save the flipped video to your phone's gallery.

you can effortlessly flip or mirror your selfie video using the CapCut app, achieving the desired result with just a few simple clicks.

HOW TO FREEZE FRAME A VIDEO ON THE CAPCUT APP

Creating a freeze-frame effect on your video using CapCut is remarkably simple. With just one click, your video can be paused for a duration that you can customize according to your preferences. Here's a detailed explanation and tutorial:

❖ **Open CapCut:** Launch the CapCut app on your Android phone and start a new project.

❖ **Add Your Video:** Select and add the video that you wish to enhance with a freeze-frame effect.

- ❖ **Choose the Freeze Part:** Decide which segment of the video you want to freeze or pause.
- ❖ **Access the Edit Menu:** Open the Edit menu at the bottom or simply tap on the video clip within the timeline.
- ❖ **Find the Freeze Option:** Search for the Freeze menu at the bottom of the screen and tap on it.
- ❖ **Insert Freeze Frame Clip:** A new clip will be inserted into the middle of the video, effectively freezing the specified segment.
- ❖ **Adjust Duration:** Finally, customize the duration of the freeze frame clip by dragging the white lines at each end of the clip.

with these steps, you can effortlessly incorporate a freeze frame effect into your video using CapCut, providing you with the flexibility to pause specific portions and enhance your video editing experience.

HOW TO ADD NEON LINE LIGHTS INTO VIDEOS IN CAPCUT

Creating a neon video effect in CapCut is incredibly straightforward. With just one click, your videos, and even photos, can be instantly enhanced with a neon glowing line effect – no need for intricate settings. Here's the step-by-step tutorial:

- ❖ **Launch CapCut:** Open the latest version of the CapCut app and initiate a new project.
- ❖ **Add Your Video:** Select and incorporate the video to which you want to apply the neon line light effect into the project.
- ❖ **Access Effects Menu:** Open the Effects menu located at the bottom of the screen.
- ❖ **Choose Party Effects:** Select the Party Effects category from the available options.

- ❖ **Apply Neon Outline Effect:** Locate the CapCut effect titled Neon Outline and tap on it.
- ❖ **Confirm and Apply:** Tap the tick button to seamlessly apply the neon effect to your video.
- ❖ **Adjust Duration:** Lastly, tailor the duration of the neon light effect according to your preferences.

By following these simple steps, you can effortlessly incorporate a captivating neon glowing line effect to your videos or photos using CapCut, enhancing your creative projects in just a few seconds.

HOW TO AUTO SUBTITLE VIDEOS ON ANDROID IN CAPCUT

Great news for video creators! There are now numerous auto-caption generator apps for Android that can significantly reduce the time spent on video editing, especially considering the lengthy process it often involves. One such app is CapCut. However, to use CapCut for auto-generated captions on Instagram and TikTok, your Android device needs to be online. Without an internet connection, you might encounter a message stating, "CapCut couldn't create auto-captions, try again later."

The tutorial for utilizing auto captions in CapCut is straightforward. Follow these steps:

- ❖ **Initiate a New Project:** Start by creating a new project on the CapCut application's home screen.
- ❖ **Add Your Video:** Incorporate the video you want to auto-caption into the editing project.
- ❖ **Access Text Menu:** Open the Text menu located at the bottom of the screen.

- ❖ **Choose Auto Captions:** Select and tap the Auto Captions option.
- ❖ **Add Captions:** Tap the "Add captions" button to proceed and confirm the automatic caption generation.
- ❖ **Select Original Sound:** In the sound options, choose "Original sound" if your video contains a narrator's voice.
- ❖ **Choose Language:** Select the language used in the video. CapCut currently supports auto captions in English, Japanese, Korean, and Portuguese.
- ❖ **Initiate Auto Captioning:** Tap the "Continue" button to start the auto-caption creation process.
- ❖ **Wait for Completion:** Wait for the auto-caption creation process to finish. The duration depends on the length of your video.
- ❖ **Batch Edit and Style Options:** Edit the caption text if needed through the Batch edit menu. Adjust font type, color, and other style elements through the Style menu.
- ❖ **Save and Share:** Finally, save the auto-captioned video to your gallery for sharing on TikTok or Instagram Reels.

HOW TO ADD A GLITCH EFFECT TO VIDEO ON CAPCUT

The glitch effect is among the most captivating features in CapCut, offering various glitch effects within the application. Surprisingly, making a video glitchy on CapCut requires just a single click. Waste no time and grasp the tutorial below:

- ❖ **Initiate a New Project:** Open the CapCut application and start a new project.

- ❖ **Add Video or Photo:** Incorporate the video or photo you intend to infuse with a glitch effect.
- ❖ **Access Effects Menu:** Open the Effects menu situated at the bottom of the screen.
- ❖ **Choose Retro Effects:** Select and tap the Retro CapCut effect category.
- ❖ **Select Glitch Effect:** Within the Retro effects, you'll discover several glitch options like Glitch, Snow Glitch, and Wavy. Choose and tap the one that suits your preference.
- ❖ **Adjust Duration:** Lastly, customize the duration of your selected CapCut glitch effect according to your preferences.

As mentioned earlier, utilizing a glitch effect in CapCut can elevate your video, making it suitable for applications like creating engaging YouTube intros.

HOW TO ADD BOUNCE EFFECT TO VIDEO IN CAPCUT

The process of adding a bounce effect to your video using the CapCut app is remarkably straightforward, requiring just a single click. Furthermore, CapCut offers more than one bounce effect to choose from. Follow the steps below:

- ❖ **Launch CapCut App:** Open the CapCut application on your iPhone or Android device and initiate a new project.
- ❖ **Add Your Video:** Select and incorporate the video to which you want to apply the bounce effect.
- ❖ **Access Edit Menu:** Open the Edit menu or tap the specific video clip on the timeline.

- ❖ **Explore Animations:** Navigate to the Animations menu by tapping on it.
- ❖ **Choose Combo Animations:** Under the Combo animation category, you'll discover two CapCut bounce effects - Bounce 1 and Bounce 2. Choose the one that fits your preferences and tap on it.
- ❖ **Adjust Duration:** Customize the duration of the selected bounce video effect according to your liking.
- ❖ **Apply the Effect:** Lastly, tap the checkmark button to apply the effect, then play your video to witness the results.

This process allows you to easily enhance your video with a captivating bounce effect using CapCut.

HOW TO MAKE BOUNCE PHOTO IN THE CAPCUT APP

You can apply a bounce effect to your photos in CapCut using an alternative method. Follow the steps below to practice this tutorial:

- ❖ **Initiate a New Project:** Create a new project and include a black or transparent image as the background.
- ❖ **Access Stickers Menu:** Navigate to the Stickers menu located at the bottom of the screen.
- ❖ **Import Your Photo:** Tap the plus sticker button to import your desired photo into the project.
- ❖ **Open Animations Menu:** Access the Animations menu within the app.
- ❖ **Apply Bounce In Animation:** In the Animation category, select the Bounce In effect and adjust the duration according to your preference.

- ❖ **Apply Bounce Out Animation:** Similarly, in the Out animation category, choose the Bounce Out effect and set the duration accordingly.
- ❖ **Finalize and Preview:** Conclude the process by tapping the checkmark button. Play the project to preview your photos after being enriched with the bounce effect.

By following this method, you can seamlessly incorporate a dynamic bounce effect into your photos within the CapCut app.

HOW TO ADD BLACK FLASH IN CAPCUT AS A TRANSITION

In CapCut, you can utilize the black flash effect as a transition between clips, creating a seamless visual transition. Follow these steps to incorporate the black flash transition into your project:

- ❖ **Initiate a New Project:** Begin by creating a new project within the CapCut application.
- ❖ **Add Media Clips:** Include two videos, two photos, or a combination of both into the project.
- ❖ **Split if Necessary:** If you've added a single video or photo, use the Split menu to divide it into two segments.
- ❖ **Access Transition Menu:** Navigate to the CapCut transition menu located at the intersection of each clip.
- ❖ **Select Black Flash Transition:** Within the Basic category, locate the CapCut black flash effect known as "Black Fade."
- ❖ **Apply Effect and Set Duration:** Select and tap the Black Fade effect, then adjust the duration according to your preference.

❖ **Apply to All (Optional):** For efficiency, use the "Apply to all" option to extend the black flash transition effect to all clip intersections.

with these steps, you can integrate the black flash transition effect, enhancing the visual appeal of your CapCut project.

HOW TO USE A BLACK OVERLAY IN CAPCUT

Apart from the initial tutorial, you can also employ the overlay method to incorporate a black flash as a video transition. This technique is particularly useful for applying a brief black flash effect to video clips with durations of 0.1 seconds and below. Follow these steps to achieve this effect:

❖ **Access the Overlay Menu:** Navigate to the Overlay menu and tap "Add overlay."

❖ **Add Black Image:** Integrate a plain black image, which can be sourced from the Stock videos menu. Alternatively, you can use a black image from the internet in case of any issues.

❖ **Adjust Size and Duration:** Enlarge the black image to cover the video beneath it and tailor the duration accordingly.

❖ **Open Splice Menu:** Access the Splice menu for further editing.

❖ **Select Overlay Effect:** Choose the Overlay Effect option and tap to apply.

❖ **Apply to Multiple Clips:** If desired, you can replicate the black flash effect across multiple clip intersections.

By following these steps, you can integrate the black flash transition using the overlay method, adding a dynamic touch to your CapCut video project.

HOW TO CREATE FLICKER EFFECT WITH BLACK FLASH IN CAPCUT

CapCut offers a versatile black flash effect that can be used to introduce a captivating flickering effect to both photos and videos. Similar to creating transitions, there are two primary methods to achieve a flicker effect, and this article will focus on one of the simplest approaches. Follow these steps to seamlessly integrate a flickering effect with the black flash in CapCut:

❖ **Access the Effects Menu:** Open the Effects menu located at the bottom of the CapCut interface.

❖ **Choose Party Effects:** Navigate to the Party Effects category within the Effects menu.

❖ **Select Black Flash:** Locate the specific CapCut effect named Black Flash and tap on it to select.

❖ **Adjust Duration:** Tailor the duration of the black flash flickering effect according to your preferences.

By following these straightforward steps, you can effortlessly incorporate a flickering effect using the Black Flash feature in CapCut, enhancing the visual appeal of your photos or videos.

HOW TO CREATE FADE IN A VIDEO IN CAPCUT

When it comes to achieving a smooth fade-in effect for your videos in the CapCut application, there are two distinct methods available. In this guide, we'll focus solely on implementing the fade-in effect through the Effects menu. Follow these steps to seamlessly integrate a fade-in effect into your video:

- ❖ **Initiate a New Project:** Begin by creating a new project directly from the CapCut app's home screen.
- ❖ **Add Your Video:** Incorporate the specific video you wish to enhance with the fade-in effect into your project.
- ❖ **Access the Effects Menu:** Navigate to the Effects menu located at the bottom of the interface.
- ❖ **Select Fade In Effect:** Within the Basic effects category, identify and choose the effect labeled "Fade In."
- ❖ **Adjust Duration:** Customize the duration of the Fade In effect according to your preferences.

you can effortlessly apply a professional and visually appealing fade-in effect to your video using the CapCut application.

HOW TO CREATE A FADE-OUT EFFECT VIDEO IN CAPCUT

CapCut's Effects menu offers a convenient way to simultaneously apply fade-out effects to your videos. Follow these steps to seamlessly integrate fade-out.

- ❖ **Access the Effects Menu:** Open the Effects menu and tap "Add effects."
- ❖ **Select Fade Out Effect:** Within the Basic category, locate and tap the "Fade Out" effect.
- ❖ **Adjust Duration:** Set the duration of the fade-out effect according to your preferences. Tap the check button to confirm your settings

HOW TO CREATE FADE-IN AND FADE-OUT AUDIO IN CAPCUT

 To add fade-in and fade-out effects to audio or music simultaneously, CapCut provides a straightforward process. Follow these steps:

- ❖ **Add Audio or Music:** Integrate the audio or music you wish to enhance with fade effects into your project.
- ❖ **Access the Fade Menu:** Tap the audio clip on the timeline and open the Fade menu.
- ❖ **Set Duration:** Customize the duration of both the fade-in and fade-out effects as desired.
- ❖ **Finalize and Playback:** Tap the check button to confirm your settings, then play the audio to experience how the fade-in and fade-out effects enhance the overall audio presentation.

By following these user-friendly steps, you can effortlessly add professional and polished fade-out and fade-in effects to both your videos and audio within the CapCut application.

HOW TO CREATE A MOTION TRACK IN CAPCUT AND MAKE CAMERA FOLLOW YOU ON VIDEO

CapCut makes motion tracking seamless and efficient. Follow these steps to apply motion tracking to your video:

- ❖ **Initiate a New Project**: Open the CapCut app and create a new project.
- ❖ **Import Your Video:** Add the video to which you intend to apply motion tracking.

- ❖ **Add a Motion Track Point:** Incorporate a text element, such as a dot, onto the video. Enlarge, change the color, and position it at the center of the video screen as your motion track point.
- ❖ **Set Keyframe at the Beginning:** Establish a keyframe at the video clip's starting point.
- ❖ **Adjust Video Motion:** Modify the video clip by panning or resizing, ensuring the tracked object remains centered on the motion track point.
- ❖ **Automatic Keyframe Creation:** As you manipulate the video clip, keyframe points are automatically generated, eliminating the need for manual additions.
- ❖ **Preview Your Video:** Play the video to observe the seamless motion tracking effect.

you can effectively implement motion tracking in CapCut, enhancing the dynamic elements of your video content by following these steps,

HOW TO CREATE A BIG HEAD EFFECT IN THE CAPCUT APP

In CapCut, achieving a comically enlarged head in your videos is remarkably simple. With just one click, you can give your head a larger-than-life appearance. Follow this step-by-step tutorial to effortlessly apply the big head effect:

- ❖ **Start a New Project:** Launch the CapCut app and initiate a new project.
- ❖ **Add Your Video:** Incorporate the video where you want to magnify your head.
- ❖ **Access the Effects Menu:** Open the Effects menu situated at the bottom of the screen.

- ❖ **Explore Facial Effects:** Select the Facial Effects option to delve into various facial manipulation effects.
- ❖ **Choose the Big Head Effect:** Navigate to the Emotions effect category and locate the Big Head effect.
- ❖ **Adjust Parameters:** Fine-tune the speed, range, and intensity of the big head effect to achieve the desired visual impact.
- ❖ **Set Effect Duration:** Finally, set the duration of the big head effect to align with the overall video duration.

you can seamlessly incorporate the big head effect into your video content, adding a touch of humor or creativity to your visual storytelling using these steps.

HOW TO FAST FORWARD VIDEO IN CAPCUT

The tutorial on how to fast-forward videos in CapCut is more or less the same as how to change the speed in CapCut in the previous article, how to do slow motion in CapCut. Here's step by step.

- ❖ Create a new project in the CapCut application and add the video you want to speed up.
- ❖ Cut the video if you only want to fast-forward the video in a certain part.
- ❖ Tap the video clip on the timeline then open the Speed menu.
- ❖ Select and tap the Normal menu option.
- ❖ Finally, set the number of times your video will speed up, the maximum that can be selected is up to 100 times.

HOW TO INCREASE THE AUDIO SPEED

Therefore, you have to create an editing project with one video or image in it first before you can add audio and increase the speed.

If you have done that, then you follow how to increase audio speed in CapCut in the tutorial and the steps below.

- ❖ Add the music or songs you want to speed up into the editing project.
- ❖ Tap an audio clip on the timeline or open the Edit menu.
- ❖ Select and open the Speed menu.
- ❖ To change your music or song back to normal, in the same way, you can slow down the audio speed to 1 time which is the normal speed point in the CapCut application.

HOW TO SLOW DOWN THE AUDIO SPEED

Therefore, you have to create an editing project with one video or photo in it before you can slow down the audio speed. Only after that, you can immediately follow the tutorial below.

- ❖ Add music, songs, or voice recordings for which you want to slow down the audio speed.
- ❖ Tap the audio clip on the editing timeline.
- ❖ Select and open the Speed menu.
- ❖ Change and slide the audio speed points to the left. You can slow down the audio speed in CapCut up to 0.1 times.
- ❖ Finally, tap the tick button and play your song to hear the result.

HOW TO MAKE INSTAGRAM REELS WITH MULTIPLE PHOTOS

Before practicing how to make Instagram Reels in CapCut below, you must prepare 12 photos and also the music that will be used.

- ❖ Create a new project in the CapCut application and add 12 photos to it.

- ❖ Change the aspect ratio of the video to 9:16 which is suitable for Instagram Reels.
- ❖ Add the music that you have prepared into the project.
- ❖ Make a beat mark on the music to make it easier during the photo editing process later.
- ❖ Cut all your photo clips right at the beat points that have been created. Especially for the 5th to 12th photo, cut it into two parts.
- ❖ Give a black-and-white filter to the first through fifth photo clips, as well as the seventh, nine, eleven, and so on.
- ❖ You can also add a zoom-out animation on all photos that you have given a black-and-white filter.
- ❖ Finally, save the finished video to the gallery and upload it to Instagram Reels.

CHAPTER NINE

CONCLUSION

In conclusion, CapCut is a powerful and user-friendly video editing app that offers a wide range of features to help you create high-quality videos. Whether you are a professional video editor or a beginner, CapCut offers an intuitive interface that makes it easy to create stunning videos.

One of the key features of CapCut is its wide range of editing tools, including filters, text, stickers, music, and more. These tools allow you to add a variety of creative elements to your videos, making them more engaging and visually appealing.

CapCut also offers advanced editing features, such as multi-layer editing, speed control, and transition effects, that give you more control over your videos and allow you to create more complex and dynamic content.

In addition to its editing features, CapCut offers a social media platform where you can share your videos with other users and get feedback and engagement. This provides an opportunity for creators to connect with other users, grow their audience, and get inspiration for their next projects.

Overall, CapCut is a versatile and powerful video editing app that offers a range of features to help you create high-quality videos quickly and easily. Whether you are a professional video editor or a beginner, CapCut is a great tool to help you bring your creative ideas to life.

INDEX

M

N

O

P

U

V

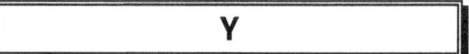

W

Y